THE 130TH ANNIVERSARY OF
JACK THE RIPPER

By
JENNIFER HELEN JOHNSTONE

CONTENTS

INTRODUCTION

This year, in 2018, marks the 130th anniversary of the notorious serial killer, Jack the Ripper. The White-chapel Murders were mainly contained to one year – 1888. Within that one year, there were a total of eight women murdered in the Whitechapel area of London. Seven of those women murdered, were women included in the Whitechapel Murder file.

There was a total of eleven women filed under the Whitechapel Murders. At one point or another, all the Whitechapel Murder victims have been linked to Jack the Ripper. Today however, only five of those women were thought to have been murdered by Jack the Ripper. These are known as the Canonical Five victims.

All of them were murdered within a short period of time. The murders of these five women, has become known as The Autumn of Terror. The Autumn of Terror happened from August the 31st 1888, until November the 9th 1888. Their names of these women were Mary Ann Nichols, who was the first woman murdered on the 31st of August 1888 by Jack the Ripper, Annie Chapman the 9th of September 1888, Elizabeth Stride and Catherine Eddowes, both were murdered on the 30th of September, and Mary Jane Kelly who was murdered on the 9th of November 1888.

There were other women murdered in Whitechapel during 1888 too, and there were two other women who were attacked in the area. The two women attacked were, Annie Millwood on the 25th of February 1888 and Ada Wilson on the 28th of March 1888. Both women were stabbed. Was this the early work of Jack the Ripper? Or, was it just a coincidence that both women were stabbed just months before Jack the Ripper killed his first victim?

Shortly after this, the first Whitechapel Murder victim, Emma Smith, was attacked on the 3rd of April 1888. She died two days later in hospital on the 5th of April 1888. There were no other murders throughout the Spring or Summer in 1888, that we know about, until Martha Tabram was murdered on the 7th of August 1888. Although Martha Tabram is not considered to be a Canon-ical Five victim, there are some good reasons why we should con-sider her to be a victim of Jack the Ripper, which we will discuss later in this book. Martha is the most contentious and controver-sial murder out of all of the victims.

Just a few weeks after Martha Tabram was murdered, another prostitute was murdered at the end of August that year. This time, a woman named Mary Ann Nichols was murdered on the 31st of August 1888.

Mary Ann Nichols is the start of the Canonical Five murders, which lasts until Mary Jane Kelly's murder in November 1888. There was only one (possible) final murder after the murder of Mary Jane Kelly, in 1888. After the murder of Mary Jane Kelly, and that was the murder? Of Rose Mylett, who died on the 20th of December 1888, which marks the end of the Whitechapel Murders in that year.

Whether Rose Mylett was murdered is up for debate, it's possible that her death was a suicide. We will look at all of the Whitechapel Murder victims in this book; including the death of Rose Mylett. We will go through a timeline of the Whitechapel Murders; particularly with the Canonical Five victims.

Once you have learned about the Whitechapel Murder and the Canonical Five victims, we will move on to other potential victims of Jack the Ripper.

Then, when you have read about the murders themselves, we are going to dedicate a chapter to what life was like in Whitechapel during 1888. Jack the Ripper gives us an insight into what life was like in London's most notorious region; Whitechapel. We may not have known what life in Whitechapel was truly like, without Jack the Ripper's atrocious murders.

The murders themselves also drew attention to the reality of Whitechapel and its citizens to the UKs media and worldwide media. Jack the Ripper drew attention to the atrocious conditions that people were living in in Whitechapel. This included elevated levels of prostitution, unemployment, poverty, homelessness, disease and squalor. Whitechapel was essentially a slum at the time and was ignored by those who were in power and wealthy, the media's attention changed that.

As we get to the middle of this book, we are going to look at the most infamous Jack the Ripper letters. Most of these were sent in October 1888, when no murders occurred. Through the letters, we get the birth of Jack the Ripper's name, from the Dear Boss letter. Before that, Jack the Ripper was referred to as Leather Apron, or the Whitechapel Murderer. Without this letter, we would not have had the name Jack the Ripper, which gave birth to an infamous legend.

There is another significant letter, the From Hell letter. The From Hell letter is significant, because it's probably the only letter which was sent by Jack the Ripper. It not only contained a letter, it also contained half a human kidney.

We then move onto the thing which is the most interesting thing about the Jack the Ripper case; the suspects. Not all of the suspects will be focused on, we will only focus on some of the main suspects, because there are literally hundreds of suspects. Therefore, there are a select group of suspects in this book.

You will then go on to read about who senior police officers who were in charge of the case at the time, thought who was Jack the Ripper. They all have different suspects; but one suspect is named more than others. You will find out who that suspect is, when you have read through this book.

To conclude this book, we are going to look at who Jack the Ripper was. Who was Jack the Ripper? Do we know who Jack the Ripper was? Several of the senior police officers at the time claimed to have known who Jack the Ripper was.

Was the Jack the Ripper mystery already solved by the police at the time and the 'mystery' which surrounds Jack the Ripper, has been a construct of our imaginations, rather than any historical facts? Perhaps.

Let's start with the timeline of the Jack the Ripper events, I hope you enjoy this book!

CHAPTER ONE: A TIMELINE OF THE JACK THE RIPPER EVENTS

Here is a timeline of the events surrounding Jack the Ripper. The events surrounding Jack the Ripper, took place from 1888 to 1891.

1888

The 25th of February 1888

Annie Millwood is attacked, she is stabbed with a clasp knife.[i] Annie Millwood was the first potential Jack the Ripper victim. She is the first woman in the Whitechapel area that was attacked in 1888. On the day she was attacked, Annie showed up to the Whitechapel Workhouse Infirmary with stab wounds all over her body. She had multiple stab wounds to her legs and torso; which has led to the suspicion that she was an early victim of Jack the Ripper.

A local newspaper called The Eastern Post, gives us an insight into the attack of Annie Millwood. An excerpt of the newspaper reads:

> *"It appears the deceased was admitted to the Whitechapel Infirmary suffering from numerous stabs in the legs and lower part of the body. She stated that she had been attacked by a man who she did not know, and who stabbed her with a clasp knife which he took from his pocket. No one appears to have seen the attack, and as far as at present ascertained there is only the woman's statement to bear out the allegations of an attack, though that she had been stabbed cannot be denied."[ii]*

It's clear that Annie's attack was like the attacks on Jack the Ripper's victims. She was attacked on her torso, much like the other victims. The attacker targeting the lower part of the body, is like that of Jack's victims in the latter half of 1888. What we do know from the later murders of 1888, is that the murders progressed to become more graphic with every murder which occurred.

It's possible that Jack started out with attacks, rather than murders. Then he progressed to murdering.

Annie initially survived the attack. She lived to confirm that she was attacked by one man, but that the man was a stranger to her.[iii] However, she died just a month later of natural causes, which wasn't related to her murder. Not much is known about Annie Millwood's attack, other than the facts stated. The only difference between Annie Millwood's attack and later Jack the

Ripper victims, is that she was attacked during daylight hours, whereas, Jack the Ripper's victims were murdered in the early morning hours of Autumn, when it would have been pitch black. It's possible though, that the Ripper was unexperienced at this point, hence the difference in the times of the murders.

Could Annie Millwood have been Jack the Ripper's first victim? It's possible. Her attack was like other victims, she was attacked by one man, in the Whitechapel area of London, she was also a similar age to the other victims (she was 38 at the time of her attack)[iv] and it's possible that she was a prostitute (all of Jack's victims were prostitutes). Are these things just a coincidence?

Possibly. But, maybe there are one too many coincidences when it comes to Annie Millwood's attack to completely rule her out as a victim of Jack's.

The 28th of March 1888

On March 28th 1888 a woman called Ada Wilson was attacked by a man while she was in her home.[v] Ada Wilson's attack was a lot more documented than Annie Millwood's. Ada describes in a lot of detail what had happened to her on the 28th of March and what her attacker looked like.

Unlike most of Jack the Ripper's victims, who were attacked and murdered outside, Ada Wilson was attacked inside. A man knocked at her door and forced his way into Ana's house. When she refused to give him money, he stabbed her twice in the throat

13

and left her for dead. Fortunately for Ana, she survived the attack and went on to describe what her attacker looked like.

She described her attacker as a young man around 30-years-old. He had a moustache, a sunburnt face and was around 5'6ft. He was wearing a hat, with light trousers and a dark coat.[vi] Ada gives us a good description of her attacker. The problem with seeing this man as Jack the Ripper is in his motivation for attacking. Jack the Ripper didn't seem to be motivated by monetary gain, whereas Ana Wilson's attacker was motivated by monetary gain. However, is it possible that Jack the Ripper was a petty thief, before he turned a violent thief and then murderer? We'll probably never know.

What is interesting, is that although the vast majority of the Ripper's murders happened outside, not all of them did. He murdered Mary Jane Kelly, one of his victims, indoors. Therefore, just because Ada Wilson was attacked indoors, doesn't mean that we should rule her out completely as a Ripper victim.

There are several reasons why we should consider Ada Wilson to be an early victim of Jack the Ripper's. First, she was attacked with a clasp knife, which was the same weapon used to attack Annie Millwood. Secondly, she may have been a prostitute, like Jack the Ripper's victims. She was also attacked in the same proximity as the other women. It's not really much to go on, but there are similarities there.

There were more similarities with the murders of Ada Wilson and the other Jack the Ripper victims, compared to our next victim;

Emma Smith.

The 3rd of April 1888

On the 3rd of April 1888, a woman named Emma Smith was brutally attacked. It is thought that Emma Smith's attack may have been the work of Jack the Ripper. This was because she was another prostitute who was attacked and murdered in Whitechapel. However, Emma Smith's murder was probably not at the hands of Jack the Ripper, as she was attacked by a gang, and not by one man.[vii] If the Ripper murders were only carried out by one man, as assumed, then Emma Smith's attack and murder must be unrelated to the Jack the Ripper murders.

What is clear though, is that Emma Smith was the first woman named on the Whitechapel Murders file. The Whitechapel Murders were eleven women who were murdered in the Whitechapel area of London, from April 1888 starting with Emma Smith, lasting until February 1891.[viii] Not all of these murders today are thought to have been committed by the same killer – Jack the Ripper.

All of the women in the Whitechapel Murders file have been thought to have been killed by Jack the Ripper at one point or another. This includes Emma Smith.

Emma Smith didn't die right away from her injuries when she was attacked on the 3rd of April. She died on the 4th of April 1888, a day after the attack happened. Her murder happened a few months before the Autumn of Terror kicked off in August 1888: when Jack the Ripper started murdering. Throughout the rest of the Spring of 1888 and most of the Summer of 1888, there were no more attacks, that we know about.

The 7th of August 1888

The next murder on Whitechapel didn't happen until the end of Summer, on the 7th of August 1888, when Martha Tabram was murdered.

Out of all the women that are named on the Whitechapel Murders file, Martha Tabram is the victim which is most contested about whether or not she was a victim of Jack the Ripper's. Some argue that Martha Tabram was killed by Jack the Ripper, while others argue that she wasn't killed by Jack the Ripper.

Before we look into whether or not Martha Tabram was a victim of Jack the Ripper's, let's look at the facts surrounding the murder of Martha Tabram.

Martha Tabram's body was found in the early morning hours of the 7th of August 1888, in George Yard Buildings in Whitechapel, by a man named Alfred Crow at around 3.30am that morning.[ix] However, it was pitch black and Alfred Crow could not see that Martha had just been murdered. He thought that she was just a homeless person sleeping on the ground, and therefore, went to his house.[x]

Martha must have been murdered sometime between 2am and 3.30am that morning, as at 2am, PC Thomas Barrett was in George

Yard Buildings and he didn't report the body of a murdered woman. He did report seeing a man waiting in the yard at this time; the man said to him that he was waiting for someone.

It's possible that either this was Martha Tabram's murderer, or, Jack the Ripper. Or, it could have been neither her murderer, nor Jack the Ripper. If it was neither, then her killer, whoever that was, must have shown up at George Yards shortly after the encounter between PC Barrett and the man he had seen.

There are several reasons why Tabram is thought to have been a Ripper victim. The first reason why she is considered to be a Ripper victim, is that she was found in the early morning hours and was murdered in the early morning hours, just like all of the Canonical Five victims were. Another reason was that she was a prostitute, just like all of the other Jack the Ripper victims.

Therefore, Martha Tabram could have been one of the early victims of Jack the Ripper. Her murder outside of the Canonical Five victims, was more likely to be the work of Jack the Rippers, than any of the other women outside of the Canonical Five victims. This is because her murder is very similar to the Canonical

Five victims, she was a prostitute, who was murdered in the early morning hours. The hours in which she was murdered, was very similar to the hours in which the Canonical Five victims were murdered.

Tabram was also murder just a few weeks before the first Canonical Five victim was murdered. Although her death technically

Jennifer Helen Johnstone

happened in the Summer, Martha Tabram's murder feels like it was part of the Autumn of Terror.

A few weeks after Martha Tabram's murder, the Autumn of Terror began. Our timeline is now going to move on to the Autumn of Terror; where most of the Jack the Ripper events unfolded.

The 31ˢᵗ of August 1888

A few weeks after Martha Tabram was murdered; Mary Ann Nichols was murdered on the 31ˢᵗ of August 1888, on Bucks Row, in Whitechapel.[xi]

On the 31ˢᵗ of August 1888, Jack the Ripper murdered his first Canonical Five victim, Mary Ann Nichols. The Canonical Five Victims were, Mary Ann Nichols, Annie Chapman, Elizabeth Stride, Catherine Eddowes and Mary Jane Kelly.[xii] The Canonical Five victims, are thought to have been the women Jack killed.

The other women who have been suspected of being killed by Jack the Ripper, the other Whitechapel Murder victims, are not thought to have been killed by Jack the Ripper. Though, this is up for debate. Mary Ann Nichols is thought to have been the first woman killed by Jack the Ripper.

Mary Ann Nichols was sometimes referred to as Mary 'Polly' Nichols, or simply, 'Polly Nichols.' It is the same woman regardless of the name.

Mary Ann Nichols was a prostitute who was out trying to earn money from the late evening hours of the 30ᵗʰ of August 1888 to the early morning hours of the 31st of August 1888. Unfortunately for Mary, she was at the wrong place, at the wrong time – during the early hours of the morning, at sometime around 3.30am, Mary was murdered at the hands of Jack the Ripper on Bucks Row.

Like all of Jack's victims, poor Mary was forced onto the dangerous streets of Whitechapel that morning. Through the pitch black, gas laden streets of Whitechapel, she was forced to seek money for a bed that night and early morning.[xiii] Unfortunately for Mary, this cost her her life.

The most tragic thing, is that Mary had already earned the money she needed for a bed, just an hour before her murder, according to Emily Holland who met her just an hour before she was murdered.[xiv]

The 8th of September 1888

Our next victim, Annie Chapman, who was murdered on the 8th of September 1888, similarly was out in the early morning hours, seeking money for a bed that evening. Unfortunately, poor Annie met the same fate as Mary Nichols.

Annie Chapman was murdered just a week after Mary Ann Nichols was murdered. She was murdered in 29 Hanbury Street, in the backyard.[xv] Annie's murder was similar to that of Mary's; she had her throat cut and was mutilated. Jack's second murder was more ghastly and gruesome than the first. Not only did he mutilate poor Annie, he disembowelled her in a more gruesome fashion.[xvi]

For a few weeks after the murder of Annie Chapman, Jack the Ripper lay low for a while. However, his silence was to be broken in the most horrific way on the early morning hours of the 30th of September 1888, when he didn't just kill once, he killed twice in that night, in the space of just an hour.

The 27th of September 1888

One of the most infamous letters in the Jack the Ripper case, the Dear Boss letter, was sent to the press on this day. The Dear Boss letter was sent to the Central News Agency in London and was signed off with the name 'Jack the Ripper.' This was the letter which gave Jack the Ripper his name[xvii], before then, the name, 'Jack the Ripper' had not been used.

If it wasn't for the Dear Boss letter, then it's possible that Jack the Ripper, could have been lost to historical obscurity. 'The Whitechapel Murderer', or 'Leather Apron', doesn't have the same chilling ring to it as 'Jack the Ripper.'

It is 'Jack the Ripper' which has created the figment of our imagination about the notorious serial killer. A man wearing a top hat, in the foggy Whitechapel streets of London. A distant man who we don't know the name or face of, but one we can see in the shadows – Jack has become a terrifying shadow figure in history.

But at the same time, it has not only kept alive the Whitechapel Murders, and the history of the Victorian slums of Whitechapel, which probably would have been forgotten, if it wasn't for Jack the Ripper. It has also created a mythical Jack, a sort of pop culture figure, which has attracted a lot of myths to the history – a top hat serial killer, in a London heavily covered in fog.

It's somewhat created a Jack that we want him to *be*, rather than one that he *was*. In other words, it has resulted in people over the years creating Jack, rather than finding out who the real Jack the Ripper was.

The 29th of September 1888

The Dear Boss letter is sent to Scotland Yard.

The 30th of September 1888

On the 30th of September 1888 the most infamous, unpredictable and eventful (in a macabre way), nights happened in the Jack the Ripper happened – Jack the Ripper strikes twice. He only killed twice on one night, and one night alone. That night was the 30th of September 1888. That night became known as the Double Event.[xviii] The two murders occurred within an hour of each other.

The two women murdered that night were, in order of them being murdered, (1) Elizabeth Stride, and then (2) Catherine Eddowes. Jack the Ripper seemed out of control that night. He almost got caught by killing Elizabeth Stride. Only just escaping, and not sickly fulfilled (he didn't get the chance to mutilated Elizabeth, as he was interrupted), he went from Dutfield's Yard, to Mitre Square.

He murdered his second victim, Catherine Eddowes, just around an hour later, inside Mitre Square. To give a sense of how out of control he must have been that night, he (a) already raise the alarm by killing Elizabeth, so swarms of police officers would have been on the streets, and (b) Mitre Square was a heavily patrolled area at the time – it is a wonder that he escaped without capture at all.

Although Jack the Ripper's fifth and final victim was the most brutal of all his killings, it was Jack the Rippers Double Event murders on the night of the 30th of September 1888, that are most intriguing. This night, perhaps more than any other night, gives us an insight into Jack.

He was out of control that night, indicating that he was probably an erratic individual, who had no control over his impulses. But someone who was also opportunistic. His murder of Catherine Eddowes clearly indicates that he was opportunistic, as he couldn't have known that he was going to come across her at that moment – she had just been released from jail shortly before hand.

There are also two other things, besides the murders themselves, which are very interesting about the Double Event. The first thing is; that there was graffiti on a nearby wall that night. That graffiti read:

'The Jewes are the men which shall not be blamed for nothing.'[xix]

It's possible that this was written by Jack the Ripper after the murder of Catherine Eddowes. However, that is not certain. We can't actually be sure who wrote this message. What is certain, is that we don't know what it looked like. No one does, apart from the person who wrote it, and the police officers who seen it. We don't know what it looked like, because it was washed off.

Given that the graffiti was washed off, and that there were no photographs taken of it, we will never know if the graffiti was in the same handwriting as one of the letters. If the graffiti matched one of the letter handwriting, then it would have been very interesting. It would have told us more about Jack the Ripper.

Once the Double Event happened on the 30th of September 1888, two police forces became involved in the Jack the Ripper case. This was because there was already one police force involved, the Metropolitan Police, at the time of the first three murders. However, the murder of Catherine Eddowes, drew the City of London Police into the case. The City of London Police investigated the murder of Catherine Eddowes, as the murder took place in their district.[xx]

The hunt for Jack the Ripper was now being pursued on two fronts, by two police forces, by , the City of London Police and the Metropolitan Police. This could have one of the reasons that Jack the Ripper lay low throughout October 1888. He didn't commit any murders, that we know about, during October 1888. Another reason he could have been laying low during this time, is because he was nearly caught that night, perhaps it made him pause.

So, maybe there was some other reason he lay low for over five weeks. Perhaps he was too ill, either mentally or physically to be able to do anything. Or, perhaps he was sickly satisfied with the murder of Catherine Eddowes. What we do know, is that he killed one final time, five weeks later. Before we get to that, let's look at the month of October and what happened there.

The 1st of October 1888

The Saucy Jack Postcard was sent to the Central News Agency in London on this day.[xxi] The Saucy Jack Postcard isn't that long, it's only a few lines long.

However, it is one of the few letters, out of hundreds of letters in the Jack the Ripper case, which have gained prominence. The reason for this, is that the postcard seems to mention the Double Event, which happened the night before.[xxii]

One clue that the Saucy Jack Postcard was a hoax, is the date on it. It was stamped with the date of the 1st of October. This would have gave the author of the postcard enough time to fabricate the postcard, to claim it was Jack the Ripper. The Saucy Jack Postcard, was signed off with the name, 'Jack the Ripper.'[xxiii]

The 4th of October 1888

On this day, both the Dear Boss letter and the Saucy Jack postcard, was published by the Evening Standard for the first time.[xxiv]

The public only became aware of the Saucy Jack postcard several days after it was dated (and sent). It was dated the 1st of October 1888, and it was published in the press a few days later, on the 4th of October 1888, which made it available to the public. This was at the height of the Autumn of Terror.

By the time that the Saucy Jack postcard was published, it was around the midway mark of the Autumn of Terror. Although, by this point, Jack had murdered four out of the five women he murdered by this point. There would however come more; one more murder and one more significant letter.

If not thee most significant letter of the time...

The 16th of October 1888

That letter was the From Hell letter, which was sent on the 16th of October 1888. The From Hell letter is also known sometimes as the 'Lusk Letter', due to the recipient of the letter – Mr George Lusk.[xxv] George Lusk was a member of the Whitechapel Vigilance Committee; a group set up by local business men in the Whitechapel area aimed at catching the Whitechapel killer.

The From Hell letter is different from all of the other letters; in two main ways.

The first way that the From Hell letter is different from all the other letters; is that it was sent to the address of a normal; Mr Lusk, rather than it being sent to a news agency, like other letters.

This makes this letter stand out. It makes it seem personal.

It seems personal, because by it being sent to Mr Lusk, it seems as if the message of the letter (and the package that came with the letter), was intend for Lusk, rather than for the press, or the police. It was certainly a letter aimed at getting attention. However, unlike the letters before it, which seem to have sought attention from the media, it seems that this letter was seeking attention from not just Lusk, but from the Whitechapel community itself.

It was saying in a roundabout way, 'I know who you are. I know that you are looking for me. I am one of you. I am within the Whitechapel community'. It was essentially trying to strike fear into the hearts of Whitechapel residents.

But is also gives us a big clue about Jack the Ripper (if this letter was written by him). He was local, he knew what was happening (the public reaction and response to his killings). But more interestingly, it suggests that he could have known Lusk personally. It makes Jack seem more real, than the shadow figure of mystery that popular culture has always thought of him.

Another interesting thing about this letter, was that it was sent with a package. That package contained something very disturbing; half a human kidney.

You will learn more about the From Hell letter, and all of the other letters later on in this book. From the From Hell letter, up to the 9th of November, nothing really happened. There were no other killings, that we know of.

The 7ᵗʰ of November 1888

One of the leading suspects, Francis Tumblety, is arrested for gross indecency.

The 9ᵗʰ of November 1888

On the 9ᵗʰ of November 1888, Jack the Ripper's silence, was to be broken in the most shocking way. He would commit his final and most brutal murder. That murder, was of Mary Jane Kelly. She was murdered by Jack the Ripper on the 9ᵗʰ of November 1888. She was murdered in Miller's Court, in Whitechapel London.

Unlike the other victims of Jack the Ripper; Mary Jane Kelly was murdered inside. Prior to this, Mary Ann Nichols, Annie Chapman, Elizabeth Stride and Catherine Eddowes, were all murdered outside. Their bodies were left on the streets. Whereas, Mary Jane Kelly was murdered in her home.

Mary was the most brutal murders out of all the five. It's as if Jack literally exploded when it came to poor Mary. She was so badly murdered and mutilated, that one person at the time even expressed, "it looked more like the work of a devil, than the work of a man.'[xxvi]Calling Jack the Devil is an accurate description of the Ripper. It was Jack the Rippers worst mutilation out of all of the victims.

Jack's last killing gives us even more insight into his psychology than previous murders. He didn't just murder Mary Jane Kelly, he was violent to the point of hatred, rage...what seems as if he was trying to completely destroy Mary's body, in the most horrible and horrific way. Suggesting that his motivation was either a hatred of women, prostitutes, or both.

This is where the Jack the Rippers murders stopped, the Canonical Five murders anyway. There were a few other murders after the murder of Mary Jane Kelly. However, today, it is thought that they were not committed by Jack the Ripper.

Potentially he had other victims that we did not know about, either during the Autumn of Terror, or before the Autumn of Terror. However, there is no evidence that he did commit any other murders. We can't rule out the possibility either.

Mary Jane Kelly might have been the last victim of Jack the Ripper. However, there were other murders linked to Jack the Ripper, murders which are included in the Whitechapel murder file.

The 20ᵗʰ of December 1888

Rose Mylett is found dead in Clarke's Yard. She was a Whitechapel Murder victim, but not a Canonical Five victim.[xxvii]It's not agreed upon how exactly she died. She either died of murder, accidental death, or suicide.

The 17ᵗʰ of July 1889

Whitechapel Murder file victim Alice McKenzie was found murdered on this day. It's been debated whether she was a victim of Jack the Ripper.

Alice McKenzie was not a Canonical Five victim, she was a Whitechapel Murder victim.[xxviii] The theory of Alice McKenzie's murder by experts, is that her murder was not by the same hands of Jack the Ripper, but the work of a copycat killer.[xxix]

She was found killed in Castle Alley.

The 10ᵗʰ of September 1889

The torso of a woman, known as the Pinchin Street Torso, is recovered under a railway arch.[xxx]

The 13ᵗʰ of February 1889

Frances Cole was found murdered.

The Closing of the Saga

The Whitechapel killings officially came to an end on the 13ᵗʰ of February 1889. It closed what was to become one of the World's biggest mysteries.

Even to this day, the Whitechapel Murders and Jack the Ripper, largely remain a mystery. Many theories about the killings, and the killer(s), have been put forward. None, so far, have proved effective in solving the mystery, and naming Jack the Ripper.

The Whitechapel Murders took place from 1888 to 1891.

Whereas, the Canonical Five Jack the Ripper murders took place from August 1888 up until November 1888. The Canonical Five Jack the Ripper murders is known as the Autumn of Terror, which is the area studied and referenced most when talking about Jack the Ripper.

CHAPTER TWO:
THE CANNONICAL
FIVE VICTIMS

The canonical five victims of Jack the Ripper were five victims which were thought to have been murdered by the same killer; Jack the Ripper.[xxxi] To clarify this, there were eleven murder victims linked to Jack the Ripper. These eleven victims, are known as the Whitechapel Murders. Experts do not think all these murders were committed by the same killer. One of the main reasons for this, is the difference in the murders.

Five of these eleven victims, were thought to have been committed by the same killer; Jack the Ripper. This is due to the similarity of the killings of all five murder victims. The five victims are now known as the Canonical Five. They were (1) Mary Ann Nichols, (2) Annie Chapman, (3) Elizabeth Stride, (4) Catherine

Eddowes and (5) Mary Jane Kelly.

Not everyone agrees that these five women were killed by Jack the Ripper. The website Casebook[xxxii] shows you how much disagreement there is about the victims, the nature of the killings, and of course, the suspects. Some people will argue that there were only three Ripper victims; Mary Ann Nichols, Annie Chapman and Elizabeth Stride.

It's argued by some that Elizabeth Stride, and Mary Jane Kelly were not victims of Jack the Ripper, because there were no mutilations on Elizabeth Stride and Mary Jane Kelly's death is quite different from the other ripper victims - her death was more brutal and gruesome.

But, there is evidence to the contrary. With Elizabeth Stride, the police at the time thought that Jack the Ripper had struck again that night; killing Elizabeth. To add to that, the coroner (Wynne Baxter) thought that Elizabeth Stride was killed by the same hands as the other two previous Jack the Ripper suspects; Mary Ann Nichols and Annie Chapman.[xxxiii]

There was a second murder after Elizabeth Stride, not too far from where she was found. That second murder was of Catherine Eddowes, who was murdered just under an hour later. What are the chances of two murders happening within a small radius, within an hour of each other, having been done by two different murderers? It's very slim. Just after Jack had killed Elizabeth (before he was going to mutilate her?), a man by the name of Louis Diemschutz probably interrupted the killer.[xxxiv]

Jack didn't appear satisfied with killing Elizabeth Stride, probably because he didn't get the chance to mutilate her. Which resulted in him seeking a second victim shortly after. Where he did kill and mutilate his second victim that night.[xxxv] We can't say for certain that Elizabeth was a victim of Jack. However, the evidence we have, points to that.

With Mary Jane Kelly however, the picture is different. There are several reasons given as to why people do not think that she was a victim of Jack the Ripper's. Such as the fact that she was much younger than the other women Jack the Ripper killed, she was only in her early 20s; whereas most of the others were in their mid to late forties. There is another reason too - the nature of her death.

Mary Jane Kelly's death was indoors; unlike the other Jack the Ripper victims who were murdered outside. Also, her death was far more brutal and gruesome than the other victims of the Canonical Five. Poor Mary Jane Kelly was mutilated beyond recognition.

There is good reason to believe that she was a victim of Jack the Rippers, though. She suffered similar mutilations to that of the other Jack the Ripper victims. She was also a prostitute, who was murdered in the early morning hours - both things, just like Jack the Rippers other victims.

There also a gradual build of brutality with Jack the Ripper's murders. His murders got worse, more violent and brutal, the more he killed. With the exception to Elizabeth Stride. But, the reason he did not progress to kill worse with Elizabeth Stride, compared to the two previous victims, Mary Ann Nichols and Annie Chapman, is what we've explained, he was interrupted with Elizabeth Stride's murder.

We can't be sure of how many people Jack the Ripper killed. He could have killed more people than we know about, we simply don't know. A whole book could be written on the victims alone; debating whether they were or were not a victim of Jack the Ripper's.

For now, though, we are going to look at the Canonical Five victims in more detail. Starting with the first Canonical Five victim – Mary Ann Nichols, who was murdered on the 31st of August 1888.[xxxvi]

Mary Ann Nichols was murdered on the 31st of August 1888, in an area of Whitechapel known as Buck's Row. She is the first Canonical Five victim and possibly the first victim of Jack the Ripper; though this is disputed. Before her murder, Mary Ann Nichols was spotted a few times on the evening of the 30th of August and the early morning hours of the 31st of August. This wouldn't have been uncommon for Mary Ann Nichols. Mary was a prostitute, which would have meant she was out late in the evening and in the early morning hours consistently. This, and the fact that she was an alcoholic, made her very vulnerable, unfortunately.

In the Autumn of 1888, in the heart of Whitechapel, it made her exceptionally vulnerable. The last night of Mary's life, on the 30th

of August 1888, there was two dock fires raging out of control in London.[xxxvii] The fires were like a scene set in the opening of a film, the fires were so bad, that they turned the London sky a blood red colour.

The dock fire was that bad that night because of the liquor that was inside of the docks. It inflamed the docks and helped the fire spiral out of control. The fires were so intense that night, that it lasted into the early morning hours. We get an insight into the fires through one of Mary Ann Nichols friend, Emily Holland, who met Mary just about an hour before Mary was murdered.

Emily was going home from the dock fires at around 2.30 am on the morning of the 31st of August 1888. That was just about an hour before Mary was killed, making Emily the last known person to have seen Mary.[xxxviii] Before we get to Mary Ann Nichols last encounter, with Emily Holland, let's look at what we know about her final hours.

We aren't aware of what Mary Ann Nichols was doing in the early evening hours of the 30th of August. It's only from 11 pm on that evening, that we are enlightened to evidence of her whereabouts. Most likely Mary was soliciting trade that evening, by 11 pm, as she was seen walking down Whitechapel Road at that time.[xxxix]

Then, at 12.30 am, on the morning of the 31st of August 1888, Mary was seen leaving the Frying Pan Public House, a pub on the corner of Brick Lane and Thrawl Street. She left the Frying Pan to return to her lodgings at 18 Thrawl Street. Mary stayed at her lodging house for around an hour.

This was until she was forced to find money for a bed. She didn't have the money. At either 1.20am or 1.40am, Mary Ann Nichols was sitting in the kitchen of the lodging house, she was told to get out, by the lodging house deputy; because she did not have the money to pay for a bed.

Mary agreed to leave the lodging house. She stood up, and as she was leaving the kitchen, she told him to keep a bed for her. Saying to him as she left, "Never Mind!" She says, "I'll soon get my doss money. See what a jolly bonnet I've got now." Mary had a new bonnet, she was showing how proud she was of having it and was sure that it would make her some money that night.

For those of you who aren't with the term "doss money", it just simply means the money for a bed at a lodging house.

As soon as she said that, Mary Ann Nichols left the lodging house. Mary was going out into the dangerous streets of Whitechapel... more dangerous that morning, with Jack the Ripper on the loose.

Around an hour later, at 2.30 am, Emily Holland, Mary Ann's friend, met Mary Ann as they were walking down Whitechapel Road and Osborn Street. Emily Holland was making her way back from the dock fires, which were still burning at that point. Emily was heading on the way home when she met Mary; whereas, Mary was wondering the streets in search for money. Money that she had already obtained that night.

When Emily met Mary that night, Mary was drunk. She said to

Emily Holland that, "I've had my doss money three times today and spent it." She says, "It won't be long before I'm back." Sadly, Mary wouldn't be back, Emily was the last person to see Mary alive (that we know of), besides Mary's killer – Jack the Ripper.

Emily described Mary as being "very drunk" when she met her. So much so, that Mary "staggered against the wall", according to Emily. The pair spoke for over five minutes when they met.

Somewhere between the time she departed Emily at around 2.40am, and 3.45 am, Mary would meet her killer - Jack the Ripper. It's unclear exactly when Mary met Jack the Ripper, but, most likely it was sometime between 3.15 am and 3.45 am on the morning of the 31st of August 1888.

We know this because of the timings of police patrols, and from the Doctor's opinion of when Mary had died. At 3.15am that morning, PC John Thain was on his patrol, he was walking down Buck's Row, where he saw nothing unusual or out of the ordinary. Then, at around the same time, Sgt Kerby also patrolled Buck's Row, he also didn't find anything out of the ordinary.

Around a half an hour later, at 3.40 to 3.45 am, Mary Ann Nichol's body was found outside the entrance to Buck's Row, by a cart driver Charles Cross, who was on his way to work that morning. Soon after, another man called Robert Paul was walking by. Charles Cross shouted over to him, saying "Come and look over here, there's a woman." Paul replied to her, "I think she's breathing...but it is little if she is."[xl]

As both Charles Cross and Robert Paul were heading for work that morning, they didn't want to be late, therefore, they went in search of the police. Before they done that, they attended to Mary. Nichols skirt was raised by Jack the Ripper. He did this so that he could mutilate her, it is thought. There were mutilations found on her body afterwards. The men lifted her skirt down, so that she would be covered, rather than being left with half of her body exposed. Then they both went and looked for the police.

Both went to go and get a police officer. Just minutes later, they returned to the scene of the murder with PC Jonas Mizen. They met PC Jonas Mizen at Hanbury Street and Baker's Row. They alerted PC Jonas Mitzen to Mary Ann's body, then went off to work. By the time that PC Mitzen arrived in Buck's Row, there were two other police officers there; PC John Neil and PC Thain.[xli] It only took a matter of minutes for several police officers to surround Mary Ann Nichols – which suggests her murder was swift.

Jack didn't hang around, it appears that he killed his victims quickly, and disappeared quickly. There is further reason to suspect this.

Once PC Thain had arrived on the scene, Thain calls for the local doctor who lives nearby, Dr Rees Ralph Llewellyn. He returned with Dr Rees Ralph Llewellyn just a few minutes later. Dr Rees Ralph Llewellyn examined the body of Mary Ann Nichols, at 3.50 am, Dr Llewellyn affirms that Mary Ann Nichols is dead, if "but a few minutes."[xlii]

In other words, Dr Llewellyn confirmed that Mary wasn't murdered that long after her body was found. It's possible that she was even still alive when Cross and Paul found her, as Paul himself said before they went to get a police officer that he thought that she was still alive.

This is one of the reasons that Charles Cross has been and is a suspect – he was found near the body of a woman that had just been murdered, and possibly still alive.[xliii] We can take a few things from Cross:

. It's suspicious that he was found near Mary Ann's body.

. He's found at the scene of a murder. Where a woman was possibly still alive when Charles Cross 'found?' her.

That's more to go on than most of the other Jack the Ripper suspects. But, questions remain.

. If Cross was the Ripper, why didn't he attack Paul and flee? Either, it's because Cross wasn't the Ripper, and genuinely did find her. Or, it gives us an insight into the Ripper's motives for killing – perhaps Jack was killing on some twisted moral crusade; in his mind.

That's only speculative though.

If Cross wasn't Jack, then he must have just missed the Ripper. Cross came from one direction, while just seconds later, Paul came of the other direction of Buck's Row. So where did Jack go?

If Cross wasn't Jack the Ripper, then the Ripper must have *just* escaped detection. If either Cross, or Paul walked down Buck's Row just minutes earlier (assuming Cross wasn't the killer), then history's most notorious serial killer could have been stopped, before he even started.

Soon after the event, Nichols body was taken to the mortuary. It's from the mortuary report that we get an understanding of what she was wearing that night; at the time of her murder. She was wearing a black bonnet (like the one she talked about in the lodging house), she was wearing a brown frock, with black wool stockings, brown stays, flannel drawers, white flannel chest cloth and two petticoats with men's boots.

Overall, it was said that her appearance was unkempt.

There were a few accessories on her body, but not many. A handkerchief, a broken mirror and a comb. No money was found on her.

This is what The Times had reported about her inquest:

> *"Five teeth were missing, and there was a slight laceration of the tongue. There was a bruise running along the lower part of the jaw on the right side of the face. That might have been caused by a blow from a fist or pressure from a thumb. There was a circular bruise on the left side of the face which also might have been inflicted by the pressure of the fingers. On the left side of the neck, about 1 in. below the jaw, there was an incision about 4 in. in length, and ran from a point immediately below the ear. On the same side, but an inch below, and commencing about 1 in. in front*

of it, was a circular incision, which terminated at a point about 3 in. below the right jaw. That incision completely severed all the tissues down to the vertebrae. The large vessels of the neck on both sides were severed. The incision was about 8 in. in length. the cuts must....

have been caused by a long-bladed knife, moderately sharp, and used with great violence. No blood was found on the breast, either of the body or the clothes. There were no injuries about the body until just about the lower part of the abdomen. Two or three inches from the left side was a wound running in a jagged manner. The wound was a very deep one, and the tissues were cut through. There were several incisions running across the abdomen. There were three or four similar cuts running downwards, on the right side, all of which had been caused by a knife which had been used violently and downwards. the injuries were form left to right and might have been done by a left handed person. All the injuries had been caused by the same instrument."[xliv]

Mary Ann Nichols was the first Canonical Five Jack the Ripper victim, but she wasn't the last victim. Just around a week later, Jack the Ripper would strike again. This time, his second victim was a woman called Annie Chapman, who was murdered about ten minutes away from where Mary Ann Nichols was found.

The second victim of Jack the Ripper was Annie Chapman. Annie Chapman was murdered and mutilated by Jack the ripper on the 9th of September 1888, in 29 Hanbury Street in Whitechapel.[xlv]

Who was Annie Chapman?

Annie Chapman was born in September 1841, the exact date of Annie Chapman's birth that month is not known. She was born named Eliza Ann Smith, to her parents, who were George Smith and Ruth Chapman.

George Smith and Ruth Chapman became married after Annie Chapman was born, they were married on the 22nd of February 1842, in Paddington.

Annie had four siblings in total, she had four sisters and one brother. Annie was the oldest of her siblings. Her other three sisters were, (1) Emily Latitia, who was born in 1844, (2) Georgina, who was born in 1856 and (3) Miriam, who was born in 1858. And finally, Annie had a brother named Fountain Smith, who was born in 1861.

At the time of Annie's parents' marriage, her father was working in the army, he was a private 2nd battalion of lifeguards. It is unknown what Annie's mother done, though, employment for women in the Victorian era was relatively scare and limited, therefore, she may not have been employed.

Married life and children

Annie Chapman married her husband on the 1st of May 1869. She was married to John Chapman, at All Saints Church in Knightsbridge, London. Her husband, John Chapman, was a coachman at the time of their marriage. They lived in several places during their marriage.

The first address that they lived in was 29 Montpelier Place in Brompton. They lived there with Annie's mother, who had lived there up until the time of her death in 1893. By 1870, Annie Chapman and John Chapman moved to 1 Brook Mews. In 1873, the had moved to 17 South Bruton Mews. And in 1881, the couple had moved to Windsor, as John got a job as a coachman.

Annie and John had three children. They were, (1) Emily Ruth Chapman born in 1870, (2) Annie Georgina Chapman, who was born in 1871 and (3) John Alfred Chapman who was born in 1880. Which means that Annie's youngest child was only around eight years old at the time of her murder.

Annie Chapman moves to Whitechapel

It's unclear when exactly Annie Chapman had moved to White-chapel, however, the first record of her being in Whitechapel in 1886. By 1886, Annie was living with a man called John Sivvey, who was a sieve, Annie had split from her husband prior to that, due to her heavy drinking. Sometime after that, she began a relationship with Sievvy.

Annie with her new man John Sivvey were living in 30 Dorset Street, which was a lodging house, in 1886. They didn't seem to live long together, as in 1886, Annie Chapman's husband died, and John Sivvy left her. It's thought that John Sivvy left her because Annie's payments from her husband had stopped.

Two years later, in May/June 1888, Annie Chapman was living in a common lodging house known as Crossingham's Lodging House, which was at 35 Dorset Street. This was just a few months before she was murdered by Jack the Ripper.[xlvi]

By the second half of August in 1888, it's clear how bad Annie's life was. She met her brother in Commercial Road in this month, saying to him that she was 'hard done by.' It's unclear what exactly made her feel that way, but, it tells us that she was down in spirits.

There are several reasons that she could have felt this way. (1) She didn't have a stable home. (2) She had a drink problem. (3) Her marriage had broken down. (4) She had become a prostitute by the time her marriage broke down. All these probably added up for poor Annie and resulted in her feeling like this in life.

On the last week before Annie was murdered, her life was turbulent.

Just around a week before her murder by Jack the Ripper, Annie Chapman was in a fight with Eliza Cooper.[xlvii] There is no exact date for when Annie Chapman and Eliza Copper had the fight, but, it's thought to have been around about the 1st of September 1888. What they were fighting about isn't exactly known either. However, there is more certainty as to what they were fighting about. It is thought that both Eliza and Annie were fighting about a man called Edward Stanley, from several witnesses at time.

There are different accounts as to what the fight was about, from the accounts of people who were there at the time. For example, it's claimed that they were fighting over the affections of Edward Stanley. This seems more possible and probable compared to Eliza's version of events.[xlviii]

Eliza claimed that the pair were fighting over a bar of soap that Annie borrowed.[1]In Victorian London in 1888, a bar of soap would have cost 6d (6 pennies).

Which doesn't seem like a lot of money to us. But one thing, we must remember the monetary value relative to the time. In other words, the monetary value of 6d would have been different to its monetary value today.

If we take other things you could buy at the time, and compare them to the soap value, what you have was - tobacco, which was also 6d, medical attendance for wife and children 3d. These two examples indicate that soap was expensive at the time, particularly if you were a poor person in the East End of London.[xlix]

As soap was expensive to a poorer person in Victorian times, perhaps there was some truth to what Eliza was saying. Regardless of the truth, it seems that there was some sort of animosity between Eliza and Annie Chapman. Although things such as having a fight over a bar of soap or potentially the affections of a lover might not raise suspicion or interest, in any other situation. But, when we have a murder inquiry on our hands, it does become relevant.

It becomes relevant because you would see Eliza Cooper as a suspect and person of interest, after the murder of Annie Chapman. Why? Not only for the animosity she shared with Annie and the fight that she had with Annie just days before her murder. But also, for what she had said to Annie during a fight in the Ringers public house.[1]

Eliza had said to Annie, according to the inquest into the murder of Annie Chapman that, *"Think yourself lucky I did not do more."*[2], this was said by Eliza to Annie after Eliza had attacked her. Now, when that is said to someone who shows up dead several days later, then we probably should automatically treat Eliza as a prime suspect.

It shows that there was a motive on Eliza's part.

Could Eliza have been responsible for Annie Chapman's death? Or, could Eliza have got someone to kill Annie several days later? Well, it's possible. It's not unreasonable to think that we should ask those things. However, we can rule Eliza out.

Just one week prior to Annie's death, Mary Ann Nichols was murdered in the same way. Both were murdered and mutilated within a week of each other. Therefore, it seems most likely that both murders are related. Eliza had a motive to kill Annie, however, there's nothing to suggest that Eliza had a motive to kill Mary.

When we think of it like this, it probably seems unlikely that Eliza had anything to do with the murder of Annie Chapman. And that the timing of her words was coincidental with the events which happened several days later – the murder of Annie Chapman.

But, there is a theory that Jack the Ripper may have in fact been Jill the Ripper.[li] Still the same questions arise though, if Eliza Cooper did murder Annie Chapman, then, why did she murder the other four suspects?

It's more than likely that Eliza was just another witness in the Jack the Ripper case. A witness which happened to say the wrong thing at the wrong time. There's nothing to suggest that Eliza Cooper was involved with any of the other murders, therefore, she wasn't Jack the Ripper.

There are only a few things that we know about Eliza, she may also have been a prostitute and her evidence at Annie Chapman's murder inquest.

This is what was recorded at the inquest:

The "Witness knew the deceased and had a quarrel with her on the Tuesday before she was murdered. On the previous Saturday deceased came in and asked the people there to give her a piece of soap. She was told to ask "Liza." Deceased then came to witness, who opened the locker and gave her a piece of soap. Deceased then handed the soap to Stanley, who went and washed himself. Deceased also went out, and when she came back witness asked her for the soap, which, however, she did not return, but said "I will see you by and by." Stanley gave deceased 2s., and she paid for the bed for two nights. Witness saw no more of deceased that night.

Witness was treated by Stanley. On the following Wednes-day witness met deceased in the kitchen and asked her to return the piece of soap. Deceased threw a halfpenny on the table and said "Go and get a halfpennyworth of soap." They then began to quarrel, and afterwards went to the Ringers public-house, where the quarrel was continued. Deceased slapped her face and said "Think yourself lucky I did not do more." Witness believed she then struck deceased in the left eye and then on the chest. She could afterwards see that the blow had marked deceased's face.

That was the last time she saw deceased alive"[lii]

Eliza lived with Annie at 35 Dorset Street, Spitalfields, White-chapel, it may have been the last time that she saw Annie alive. But, there were also several other people who saw Annie Chapman alive before her death.

We don't know much else about Annie Chapman's last week. That is, until the final few hours of her life. On the 4th of September, Annie Chapman met Amelia Palmer and gave her some money.[liii] Amelia Palmer was another witness during the Annie Chapman murder inquest. Amelia said she saw Annie several times throughout the week, between the 1st of September and the 8th of September, when Annie died, and said that Annie wasn't feeling well.[liv]

It was apparent that Annie Chapman wasn't eating, probably due to a lack of money. Sadly, Annie was in a poorly state for the last week of her life, before her tragic ending.

The Last Hours Of Annie's Life

The last hours of Annie Chapman's life, is the most documented hours of her life. For this reason, we have a good idea of most of the last hours of her life.

The last hours of her life played out in early and late evening hours of the Friday. It was the 7th of September 1888 and the early morning hours of the Saturday, the 8th of September 1888. That evening starts a 5PM. At 5PM on the evening of the 7th of September 1888, Annie Chapman is seen by Amelia Palmer in Dorset Street.[lv]

Not only do we know that Annie was poorly by this point, we also are enlightened to one of her last words. Before parting with Amelia, Annie said to her, *"I must pull myself together and go out and get some money or I shall have no lodgings."*[lvi]

What Annie was saying in other words, is that she was going out onto the streets to solicit trade, so she could have a bed for the night. What we don't know is where exactly she went and who she spent time with after she said this, for a few hours.

Both of those things are probably irrelevant anyway. It's unlikely that she met Jack the Ripper then. Given that the Ripper didn't seem to take risks on when he murdered. His murders seemed to be over quickly, according to the evidence we have. That suggests that Jack the Ripper didn't waste time between finding his victim and killing his victim.

We know roughly when Annie was murdered, due to the autopsy report and the eye witness accounts of Annie that night. One witness, Amelia, last saw her, and 11.30PM that night, when she returned to her lodging house. Annie had been out on the streets of Whitechapel prior to that. At around this time, Annie asked for permission to go inside the lodging kitchens.[lvii] She spent around 40 minutes there.

Forty minutes after Annie Chapman had entered her lodging house kitchen, after asking for permission to enter it, she was joined by another lodging house member called Fredrick Stephens. Fredrick Stephens says that he was drinking with Annie Chapman at 12.10AM, in the early morning hours of the 8th of September.[lviii]

According to Mr Stephens, Annie Chapman was already drunk and was worse for wear with the drink when he saw her at that time. It's obvious that Annie Chapman had found the money that night she was looking for, to use it to pay for her bed that night. However, she used it to buy drink.

Just two minutes after Mr Stephens joined Annie Chapman in the lodging kitchens, they were joined by another lodging house member. This lodging house member joined them at 12.12AM, his name was William Stephens.

According to Annie, she had received 5d (5 pennies) from her family earlier that day, after visiting them in Vauxhall.[3] However, it is unclear whether this is true, as she had stated to Amelia Palmer earlier that she didn't have any money.

Either Annie got her money from her family, or from soliciting trade, it's not really clear which one. What we do know, is whatever way she accumulated the money, it seems obvious that she spent that money on drink. Therefore, she spent the money she had for a bed on drink, and therefore, had to go back out onto the streets to make more money that evening.

Annie left the kitchen shortly after Stephens joined them. We don't really have any idea where she went, and who, or if she was with anyone as she left the lodging house around 12.12AM. A short time later, at 1.35AM, Annie returned back to the lodging house, where she went to the kitchen again.

This was to be her last time in the kitchen, and in the lodging house. At this time, she was sitting in the lodging kitchens eating a baked potato.[lix] Around that time, the night watchman of the lodging house, John Evans, had come into the kitchen to fetch Annie, to pay for her bed. As Annie did not have the money for her bed, she had to go up to see the lodging house deputy, Tim Donovan.

Tim Donovan is one of the people who has been named as a Jack the Ripper suspect.[lx] Donovan as Jack the Ripper seems to rest on the fact that he knew Annie Chapman, there doesn't seem to be much else to go on with Donovan as the potential Ripper – there isn't strong enough, if any evidence that suggests that Tim Donovan was Jack the Ripper.

Although, that's not to say he was a warm and cuddly character either. He was pretty harsh in the way that he dealt with Annie Chapman several hours before her death. What we should remember is, is that his behaviour wasn't out of character for a person of the time.

In other words, he was a product of his time. The harsh reality of Victorian life presented a huge gap between the rich and poor. And those who were poor, were treated pretty rough and unfairly. Which is what happened to Annie that night. Annie went upstairs to see Tim, because she didn't have the money for a bed that night.

It's estimated that she went upstairs at around 1.35AM. Going into Tim's office, Annie says to him, *"I haven't sufficient money for my bed,"*[lxi] she goes onto say, *"but don't let it. I shall not be long before I'm in."* This is met with Tim's reply, *"You can find money for your beer and you can't find money for your bed."*

From this we can gather that it was probably a regular occurrence for Annie not to have a bed, and probably spend that money on alcohol.

Annie didn't disagree with him, which further emphasises that point. She left the office and stood outside it, to which she replied to him *"Never mind, Tim." "I'll soon be back."*

The she replied to Mr Evans, *"I won't be long, Brummy* (his nickname). *See that Tim keeps the bed for me."* Soon afterwards, Annie left the lodging house. Poor Annie was forced to go out into the dangerous Whitechapel streets in those early morning hours.

Whitechapel was notorious for its danger, with gangs and violence rife. Prostitution was also rife, and it could be a dangerous place working on the streets, especially when there was a Ripper about. Prior to this night, two murders had already occurred, that of Maratha Tabram,[lxii] who was seen as the first victim of Jack the Ripper at the time, some still see her as the first Jack the Ripper victim. And, the second murder which had occurred, was Mary Ann Nichols, just a week prior to Annie's murder.

Of course, we have the knowledge of hindsight as to what happened with Annie Chapman. No one in that lodging house, unless the killer resided there, could have known what was going to happen to her when she left that lodging house. Although, at the same time, she was forced out onto the street when she was ill.

It's unclear where exactly Annie Chapman went to in her final hours, we don't know. There is no documentation of her final hours between when she left the lodging house at 1.35AM, until her body was found at around 5.30AM. What is clear, is that somewhere between that time, she met Jack the Ripper, her killer.

Annie's murdered, and mutilated body was found in the yard of 29 Hanbury Street, Whitechapel. Forty-five minutes before her body was found, a man named John Richardson entered the same yard.[lxiii] He sat outside to remove a piece of leather from his shoe. He said that he didn't see anything unusual at the time.

We should remember that at this time in the morning. It was an early Autumn morning, it would have been pitch black at the time that John Richardson went outside. Had Annie's body been lying there when John Richardson went out, he may not have seen it. Or, she might still have been alive at that time, and her body wasn't there.

This is according to the witness statement of Mrs Elizabeth Long. Mrs Elizabeth Long claimed to have saw Annie Chapman outside of 29 Hanbury Street, with a man at 5.30am. Perhaps Mr Richardson just missed Annie and the Ripper.

The man asked Annie, 'Will you?', to which Annie replied, 'Yes.' Could this have been Jack the Ripper? It probably was Jack the Ripper and Annie Chapman, given that her body was found just shortly after this discussion was held.

According to Mrs Long, the time was 5.30am, she remembered that because of the bell toll of the church tower. However, could she have been mistaken, with the time actually being 5.15am? This is because, at roughly the same time, a man called Albert Cadosch went into the backyard of 27 Hanbury Street and heard a voice from 29 Hanbury Street yard (where Annie Chapman's murdered and mutilated body was found shortly afterwards). All that Cadosch could make out, was a woman's voice saying 'no!'

The voice was most likely that of Annie Chapman's. Albert Cadosch then heard a thud on the fence. This thud was likely Jack the Ripper murdering Annie Chapman, though, unknown to Albert

Cadosch at the time, as he could not see over the fence. Cadosch couldn't make out anything else which was said, he thought nothing of what he had heard and went on his day.

Just under 30 minutes later, just before 6am, the murdered body of Annie Chapman was found by a man called John Davis. John Davis lived in 29 Hanbury Street, he was a cart driver who was making his way down stairs seen the back door open, which is when he found Annie's body.[lxiv]

A man who lived in Hanbury Street called Mr Davis, had woke during that night between 3.00am and 5.00am, but he went back to sleep.[lxv] He said that he didn't hear anything unusual and then went back to sleep. Then, he woke up later that morning at 5.45am, he went down stairs and went into the backyard to find Annie.[lxvi]

Once Albert Cadosch had found the body of Annie Chapman, he went to the police station to report the crime. Annie had become the second canonical victim of Jack the Ripper's. Her murder and mutilation was worse than the murder of Mary Ann Nichols. But, the murder of Annie Chapman wasn't the last murder by Jack the Ripper.

For a while, the murders had seemingly stopped for a while. There were no murders for a few weeks after the murder of Annie Chapman. But what was to happen next, would rock Whitechapel and the whole London establishment to its core, even more so than it had already done to this point.

Jennifer Helen Johnstone

Why?

This is because of what happened on the night (early morning), of the 30th of September 1888. On the 30th of September 1888, Jack the Ripper lost control. He didn't only murder one woman that night, he murdered two women that night. This was known as the Double Event. The first victim he murdered that night, was Elizabeth Stride.

Elizabeth Stride

Elizabeth Stride was the first of two women who were murdered on the night of the 30th of September 1888, this event was known as the Double Event.[lxvii]

Elizabeth Stride's last hours came on the 29th of September 1888, and partly on the 30th of September 1888. Unlike the two ripper victims murdered before her, and the two ripper victims who were murdered after her, Stride was murdered quite early that morning.

Most of the other murders happened between 3.30am and 5am, whereas, Elizabeth was murdered just before 1am that morning. Why Jack changed his habits that night, we will never know. Perhaps he was just an opportunist, the opportunity presented itself for him, and the outcome was devastating – the death of Elizabeth Stride.

The last hours of Elizabeth Stride's life are somewhat documented; they were the most documented of her life. We have several eye witness accounts of where she was that night and who she was with. The first account of her last hours, comes on the 29th of September 1888, at 6.30pm. This was just around six hours before she was murdered.

At that time, Elizabeth Stride was seen drinking in the Queen's Head Public House, by Elizabeth Tanner.[lxviii] They both drank in the public house and then went to their lodging house shortly after 6.30pm.

Elizabeth is then seen leaving the lodging house sometime between 7pm and 8pm, by two people called Catherine Lane and Charles Preston. She talks with them both briefly, asking Charles if she could borrow the brush he had for his clothes and asking Catherine to look after a piece of velvet that she had. According to Catherine:

"I know the deceased had 6d when she left, she showed it to me, stating that the deputy had given it to her."

It's likely that she spent the money later on drink, as the money wasn't recorded as being found on her. Of course, it could have either been given to the ripper, or took by the ripper. However, given that the ripper quickly pushed her to the ground before he murdered her and was interrupted while he was murdering her, it seems more likely that the money she had, was spent on drink.

The next few hours beyond 8.30PM that night, is a mystery. It's unknown where exactly Elizabeth Stride was between the hours between 7/8PM and 11PM on her final night. Elizabeth was spotted at 11PM. She was seen by two men, J. Best and John Gardner as they were going into the Bricklayer's Arms Public House.[lxix]

They spotted her nearby, she was near Commercial Road. Elizabeth wasn't alone though, she was seen with a man, by two men. The two men who were going into the Bricklayer's Arms Public House, were close enough to Elizabeth Stride that they got a good look at the man. They described the man with distinguishing looking features, sandy coloured eye lashes and a dark moustache.

Neither Elizabeth Stride nor the man that she was with, might have said something to the two men who were entering the Bricklayer's club – we don't know exactly what Elizabeth Stride and the man said to the two men. What we do know, is that the two men asked the mysterious man to come into the club to have a drink with them. The man refused to do so.

When the man refused to join both, they decided to go into the club themselves. Before they went into the pub, they joked to Elizabeth, *"That's Leather Apron getting 'round you."*[lxx]Leather Apron was one of the names given to Jack the Ripper. People didn't refer to Jack the Ripper, as Jack the Ripper at that point. We have to remember these murders in context as they were and try and remember that people didn't know certain things at specific times. Such as the name given to the killer – Jack the Ripper.

By the time of Elizabeth Stride's murder, Jack the Ripper wasn't a term used to describe the ripper murders. The term Jack the Ripper, came about first as a result of one of the ripper letters which were sent to the police. That letter, is the Dear Boss letter.[lxxi]

The Dear Boss letter was only sent to the police on the 29th of September 1888. It is a significant letter in this context, because the Dear Boss letter is the first time that we hear about the name Jack the Ripper. Before the name Jack the Ripper was born, people referred to the killer as 'Leather Apron.' So, who was Leather Apron?

Leather Apron was a man who was accused of coming the Whitechapel Murders, during the height of the Whitechapel killings. Local prostitutes were also fearful of Leather Apron. It is thought that he got his name from the same prostitutes. They didn't know who he was or what his name was and could only identify him by one thing; the leather apron that he would wear.[lxxii] Hence were he got his name.

Just a few weeks before the murder of Elizabeth Stride, the Star newspaper ran an article on Leather Apron. Here is an excerpt of that story that the Star ran on the 5th of September 1888:

"LEATHER APRON."

"THE ONLY NAME LINKED WITH THE WHITECHAPEL MURDERS. A NOISELESS MIDNIGHT TERROR."

The Strange Character who Prowls About Whitechapel After Midnight - Universal Fear Among the Women - Slip-

*pered Feet and a Sharp Leather-knife. The mystery attend-
ing the horrible murders in Whitechapel shows no sign of
lessening. The detectives at work on the case, who were
quick to confess themselves baffled, only continue to make
the same confession, and there is every prospect that the
last ghastly tragedy will go unpunished like its predecessors.
Whitechapel is loud in its indignation over the inefficiency
of the detectives, and is asking several questions to which
there does not seem to be any satisfactory answer. Among
other things the people wish to know why the police do not
arrest "Leather Apron."[lxxiii]*

From the start it seems a bit sensationalist, particularly to a modern reader that didn't have to live through the events in 1888. However, it gives us an insight into the fear of local residents at the time of the murders. They had to walk the same streets as a man that was somewhat a shadow figure to them, because they did not know who he was.

Further to this, the same Whitechapel residents could have been passing this murderer, or working alongside him, and wouldn't even know about it. Chances are, that someone who read this newspaper article, might have passed the ripper without even knowing it. Or worked alongside the ripper without even knowing it. Given that the ripper was highly active throughout the area, it's more than likely that he passed many people.

That would be something that he would know, but not something that ordinary members of the public would have known. When we think of Jack the Ripper like this, we realize just how much of a ghost figure that exists. Which is how we can understand the men's comments about Leather Apron, towards Elizabeth Stride. Elizabeth and the strange man went off away from the club just after 11PM.

Naturally you would assume that the man she was with, must be her killer. It must be Jack the Ripper! She is seen with this man just short of two hours before she was murdered. So, that's him? That must be the man we are looking for?!

Well, in theory, he would be seen as a prime suspect. But, considering what comes next, it's unlikely that this man was Jack the Ripper. For two reasons. Firstly, it seems unlikely that Jack the Ripper would wait almost two hours to kill Elizabeth Stride. That's because Jack the Ripper seems to have murdered quickly and got out of the crime scene quickly. We know this through his other murders, were it seems that he killed quickly and fled the scene of the crime quickly.

By quickly, we mean less than 20 minutes. Perhaps with the exception of Mary Jane Kelly. Given that this man could have been with Elizabeth Stride for 45 minutes, he had more than enough time to kill Elizabeth and flee. It seemed like a more ideal for someone as twisted as Jack, than what actually happened to Elizabeth Stride.

The other reason that this man likely wasn't Jack the Ripper, is through the description of him. The description given of him, was different than the one given about the man seen with Elizabeth Stride, shortly before her murder. Before her murder took place, at 11.45PM, Stride was seen again after disappearing with the man outside the club.

This time, Elizabeth Stride was with another man. We know this because of William Marshall, who said that he seen Elizabeth with a man on Berner Street. The man who Elizabeth was with, said to her that *"You'd say anything but your prayers."*[lxxiv]

This that was said to Elizabeth could be interpreted in several ways but sounds most likely as a taunt or a joke. It probably shouldn't be read into too deeply, as this man was probably not Jack the Ripper. Although, we cannot rule that out with certainty, since we don't know who the ripper was. Therefore, the ripper could be anyone.

But, there's good reason why we should probably rule this man out. And that is, he was not the last person seen with Elizabeth Stride that night. There was one more sighting of Elizabeth Stride that night, or early morning, before she was attacked as she was seen after midnight on the 30th of September 1888. This was shortly before the attack which occurred just 10 minutes later.

At 12.35AM on the morning of the 30th of September, Elizabeth Stride is seen by PC William Smith beside Berner Street and across from the International Working Men's Educational Club. There isn't an in-depth description of the man, not of his face anyway.

All we know is that he was almost 30 years old, around 28, he was wearing a deer stalker hat and a dark coat. The man was also carrying a parcel which was wrapped in some newspaper.[lxxv]

Could this man have been Jack the Ripper? Is this the culprit we have been looking for for almost 130 years? Well, it's possible.

It's possible for two main reason. The first, Elizabeth was killed just shortly afterwards, which makes this man a strong person of interest. Secondly, this man was seen by a credible witness – a police officer. Both of these things make this person, whoever he was, a prime suspect. However, there is nothing to say that the man who was standing on Berner Street with the package, shortly before the death of Elizabeth Stride, was Jack the Ripper. It is debated to this day who this man was.

And, it is debated to this day whether or not he was Jack the Ripper. All that we can say is, that he could have been the killer. We do have one witness though, according to a Home Office file. That witness was Israel Schwartz, who saw a man and a woman (who was probably Elizabeth Stride), on Berner Street.

The file says that Mr Schwartz was coming into Berner Street from Commercial Road at around 12.45am, this was just fifteen minutes before the dead body of Elizabeth Stride was found. He saw the man and woman talking in the gateway leading to the Dutfield's Yard, where Elizabeth was found just several minutes later. According to Mr Schwartz, Elizabeth was waiting besides the gate just outside the yard, the man stopped to talk to Elizabeth.[lxxvi]

Is this evidence that the killer knew his victims and that the victims knew their killer, because Elizabeth Stride was waiting there? As Elizabeth Stride was a prostitute, she probably would have done this several times, perhaps they were on the same spot even and others were on different spots.

That, alongside the fact that the man attacked Elizabeth quickly, probably states that she didn't know him and that he was being opportunistic in his attack. It doesn't seem as if the attacker really made an effort to try and take Elizabeth anywhere else to kill her. Which, perhaps suggests that the killer wasn't a wealthy individual luring the suspects to their deaths with grapes – a theory that has been presented.

We also know that he was opportunistic of his next victim, Catherine Eddowes. As she had previously been let out of jail at the same time he was murdering Elizabeth Stride, he couldn't have possibly known Catherine Eddowes was being released from jail, remember, this was an era without any technology really.

Therefore, it is clear that he was being opportunistic with Catherine Eddowes, most likely with Elizabeth Stride too. As with his other three victims, Mary Ann Nichols, Annie Chapman and Mary Jane Kelly, it's more difficult to tell.

This is what happened to the attack on Elizabeth Stride, according to Israel. It's probably the most detailed description that we have of any of the attacks, at least when it comes to eye witness accounts. The man tried to drag her out into the street, turning her around, he threw her to the ground. Then, Elizabeth screamed three times.[lxxvii]

Across the street looking towards them, was a man standing

lighting his pipe. The man who was lighting his pipe was shouted at by the man who was attacking Elizabeth, 'Lipski!', he cried out. At that point, Mr Israel Schwartz went off. The man shouting 'Lipski' was probably Jack the Ripper.

We know this because later when it came to identify the body of Elizabeth Stride, Mr Schwartz confirmed that Elizabeth was the woman that he saw. Given that Elizabeth Stride was found just minutes later, the man who was attacking her, he must have been her attacker, he must have been Jack the Ripper. The odds of someone else killing her after this attack seem exceptionally slim. Although, not impossible.

One more thing about Miss Stride's murder, and that it seems to be a murder which is most contested. Elizabeth Stride seems to be the most contested Canonical Five ripper victim. This seems to be because unlike the other victims, she wasn't mutilated, only her throat was cut. For this reason, some theorists claim that she was not a victim of Jack the Ripper. There are good reasons to dismiss this theory though.

Elizabeth has so many other similarities with the other Jack the Ripper victims. For example, she was a prostitute, she was a similar age to the other victims, she had dark hair like the other victims, she was killed in the early morning hours, her throat was cut, which is how Jack started his attack on his other victims. These all indicate that she had the same killer as the other Canonical Five victims.

And, we know why she wasn't mutilated – the killer was disturbed. He was disturbed around 1am, by Louis Diemschutz. When he was trying to turn into Dutfield's Yard, were Elizabeth's dead body was found by him. The ripper was thought to have still be in the yard when Louis entered the yard. This was according to Louis, who thought that he was still there. The horse seems to confirm this, as the horse refused to go forward into the yard - startled at the killer in the yard. The Ripper was almost caught.

One question does arise, how did it take Elizabeth's attacker so long to kill her and not mutilate her? If we say that she was attacked at a quarter to 1am, that he threw her to the ground and shouted 'Lipski' at the man opposite, it would have taken a few minutes at most to throw her to the ground and say that. Probably a few seconds.

We know that Jack the Ripper killed his victims quickly, with the post mortems and timings of the other victim's police patrols. That short time was around 15 minutes. It took Jack roughly 15 minutes to attack and mutilate his victims. Therefore, he had just about the right time to do what he done with the other victims, so, why didn't he?

Does this conclude that the man attacking Elizabeth Stride wasn't her killer after all? Could the killer have actually been the man on the opposite end of the street? If Elizabeth's attacker ran off and the man with the pipe waited until he did, walked over, attacked Elizabeth and slit her throat...then it would make more sense with the timing. It would make more sense that the man opposite the street was the ripper.

This would indicate that Elizabeth Stride was possibly attacked by one man, then another man attacked her (Jack the Ripper), and killed her.

Could it therefore be, that the man with the pipe was Jack the Ripper and not the attacker? We don't know who pipe man was. But, what we do know, is that he chased Schwartz, then went back to the scene. Why would this pipe man do this? Was he simply just anti-Semitic, like Elizabeth Stride's attacker was? The lipski comment from the attacker was anti-Semitic.

If so, why didn't the pipe man return to see whether or not Elizabeth was okay when he returned to the scene? Where did the pipe man go after returning to the scene? Could the pipe man chased off Schwartz, then walked back across the street and killed Stride?

When we think of it like this, the situation does seem odd and doesn't add up. There is something strange about pipe man. For Schwartz he didn't know whether or not these two men were working together,[lxxviii] he also thought that what he was witnessing was a domestic dispute.[lxxix]

Whatever was the truth with that attack, the attacker and the pipe man, is open to interpretation and discussion. It's certainly an interesting part of this case, which opens up different questions about the nature of Elizabeth Stride's murder, and the possible nature of Jack the Ripper himself, (or, their self)?

Whatever the truth, it's clear that Jack the Ripper did not strike only once that night, or, early morning, if you want to be specific about it. He struck twice that night. His second victim that night was Catherine Eddowes. Catherine Eddowes, was released from jail at the same time that Louis Diemschutz found Elizabeth Stride in Dutfield's Yard.

Before we get to Catherine Eddowes though, let us round up Elizabeth Stride. Mr Diemschutz went into the International Working Men's Educational Club just after he had found the body of Elizabeth Stride. The International Working Men's Educational Club was right next to where the body was found. It was a risky place for Jack to strike.

It was a busy club that night, which was just about to empty, with all those inside coming out onto the streets of where Jack was. This perhaps emphasizes that Jack's quest for blood that night, was so great, that he wasn't willing to take a huge risk that night not once, but twice. The second huge risk that night, was in him murdering Catherine Eddowes.

Catherine Eddowes was murdered in Mitre Square, a square which was heavily policed. On top of that, the police were already alerted to the murder of Elizabeth Stride, by the time that Jack went onto murder Catherine Eddowes.[lxxx]

Which means that there would have been a lot more police actively looking for the killer at that point. He evaded capture twice that night, not really through skill, he evaded capture that night with extreme luck. While the ripper was fleeing Dutfield's Yard and making his way towards Mitre Square, Dr. Frederick Blackwell arrived on the scene of the crime where Elizabeth Stride was killed.[lxxxi]

He arrived at 1.16am and he confirmed that Elizabeth was dead.[4] More details of her murder would arise at the post mortum and inquest on a later date.

The second woman murdered that night by Jack the Ripper, Catherine Eddowes, had quite an eventful night. We don't know much about what happened in Catherine Eddowe's life throughout the day on the 29th of September 1888. This would be her final full day. We know more about what happened throughout the evening on the 29th of September 1888, starting at 8pm.

At around 8pm on the 29th of September, Catherine was on 29 Aldgate High Street, she was drunk and surrounded by a crowd of people. Catherine is found at this time by PC Louis Robinson, she couldn't move because she was too drunk and wasn't able to move. No one knew who Catherine was when Louis ask the crowd if anyone knew who she was. PC Louis tried to get Catherine to stand up and place her against the wall.

However, she couldn't stand up, she was too drunk that she was unable to stand up. When she was placed on the wall, she fell back down again. It was at this point,

that PC Louis realized that she could not be left on her own out on the street, that she had to be taken to safety. That safety was taking her to the police station for her to sober up, as he didn't know where she lived. It wasn't until another police officer came along, PC George Simmons, that they could both take Catherine to the local police station.

That local police station was known as Bishopsgate Police Station. The two police officers left the scene at about 8,30pm that night and arrived at Bishopsgate Police Station at around 8.45pm. They arrived at the police station and Sergeant James Byfield recorded the arrival of Catherine Eddowes. When she was asked what her name was, Catherine Eddowes replied *'Nothing.'*

Ten minutes later, at 8.50pm, PC Robinson put Catherine Eddowes in her cell. She was put in the cell so that she could sleep off her drunkenness and sober up, something which did happen a few hours later. Catherine slept for just over two hours, she was awake by 12.15am, as she was heard singing in her cell. Otherwise, she remained pretty quiet.

Until 12.30am, that is when she asked when she could be released from jail. She asked when she could be released. The reply she got was, *"When you are capable of taking care of yourself."* Hutt replied. To which Catherine replied that *"I can do that now."*[lxxxii]

All went quite for the next 25 minutes.

Then, at 12.55am, PC Hutt was instructed to see if there were any persons who were ready to be released, by Sergeant Byfield. By that point, Catherine was sober enough to be released and it was decided that she would be released. Before she was released, Catherine Eddowes was asked some details about herself.

She gave her name as Mary Kelly. An ironic and weird twist of fate, is that Jack the Ripper's next victim, was Mary Kelly. A strange coincidence. Just before leaving the police station, Catherine Eddowes said her last known conversation:

"What time is it?" she asks Hutt.
"Too late for you to get anything to drink." he replies.
"I shall get a damn fine hiding when I get home." She tells him.
Hutt replies, *"And serve you right, you had no right to get drunk."*
Hutt pushes open the swinging door of that station.
"This way missus," he says, *"please pull it to."*
"All right"' Kate replies, *"Goodnight, old cock."*[lxxxiii]

It's estimated that Catherine Eddowes would have took around ten minutes to walk from Bishopsgate Police Station to Mitre Square. However, it did not take Catherine Eddowes just around 10 minutes to walk to Mitre Square. What happened to her during the 30 minutes is impossible to tell. Perhaps that she stopped to talk to someone, or that she was looking for money for drink. Either way, what we do know, is that at some point, Catherine Eddowes met Jack the Ripper shortly after leaving the police station.

It is thought that Catherine Eddowes was seen at 1.35am, just ten minutes before her murdered and mutilated body was found. She was seen at 1.35am by Joseph Lawende, Joseph Levy and Harry Harris saw Catherine with a man at the corner of Duke Street and Church Passage, which was the way into Mitre Square.

Just ten minutes later, Catherine Eddowes body was found in the corner of Mitre Square murdered and mutilated. At 1.45am, PC Edward Walkins finds the body. It must be noted that the square was checked just around fifteen minutes beforehand, and nothing seemed out of the ordinary. This square was heavily patrolled and policed.

The patrols would take place every fifteen minutes or so. It's more than likely that Catherine Eddowes met her end sometime between 1.35am and 1.45am that morning, on the morning of the 30th of September 1888. Just minutes later, PC Watkins alerted the police to the murder of Catherine.[lxxxiv] By this point, when PC Watkins raised the alarm, Jack the Ripper didn't just have one police force on his back. He had two.

By murdering Catherine Eddowes in Mitre Square, the ripper drew the City of London police into the investigation. This is because it happened within the City of London police district. And, he also had the Whitechapel police on him. Therefore, the City of London police had now also gotten involved in the hunt for the ripper.[lxxxv] After Jack the Ripper had murdered Catherine Eddowes, he was on the run again, this time, it is thought that he was running back into Whitechapel.[lxxxvi]

It's clear that Jack the Ripper was going back into Whitechapel, because of the path that he had took that night. There is one reason that we know he took this direction, even if we don't know the exact route he took – he left a clue. That clue was a blood-stained cloth, that cloth was a piece of apron from Catherine Eddowes.[lxxxvii] It's clear that Jack the Ripper was going back into Whitechapel.

The apron was found at 2.55am, around an hour after the murder of Catherine Eddowes. The distance between Mitre Square and Goulston Street makes you wonder why he took that route. It's a walk that would probably take around 20 minutes to reach, however, the apron wasn't in Goulston Street at 2.20am, according to PC Alfred Long. It was found at 2.55am by 2.55am.

It's possible that the ripper lay low for a while, or stopped somewhere, like an open building or close. But, if he did, why did he not just discard of the apron there, rather than going out onto the streets again and later doing it. Perhaps he thought it would be safer if he waited to disregard it, as it would leave a trace of where he was and going.

Maybe it indicates that Jack had a health problem, or maybe he was just exhausted. Or confused, if he had a mental illness? The list of questions are endless and speculative. It's impossible to tell really what happened that night.

The speculation has led to doubts surrounding the source of the apron. It's thought that the source of the apron was Catherine Eddowes; it was Catherine Eddowes apron. However, not everyone is convinced that the apron was from Catherine Eddowes.

This statement was given by Dr Brown at Catherine Eddowes inquest, on the 4th of October 1888:

"......My attention was called to the apron - it was the corner of the apron with a string attached. The blood spots were of recent origin - I have seen a portion of an apron produced by Doctor Phillips and stated to have been found in Goulston Street. It's impossible to say it is human blood, I fitted the piece of apron, which had a new piece of material on it, which had been evidently sewn on to the piece I have - the seams of the borders of the two actually corresponding - some blood and apparently faecal matter was found on the portion found in Goulston Street"[lxxxviii]

What we can take from Doctor Brown's statement at Catherine Eddowes inquest, is that he is saying that from the apron was found, there was a piece of apron missing from Catherine Eddowes body and that there was blood on the apron, which he cannot say is human. This is because they didn't have the technology at the time to determine whether the blood was human or animal.

It seems to me as if Doctor Brown is only uncertain about the authentication of the blood. In that he doesn't know if it is human blood, or if it is animal blood. What we should do, since we cannot examine the evidence today, is ask yourself the likelihood of this being Catherine's apron? Is it even possible that we can truly know that this apron was from Catherine, given that we cannot physically examine it?

It was an apron found just after her murder, with blood on it. That doesn't mean that it belonged to Catherine. There could have been another explanation for it. However, a piece of apron was missing from her body, one that fitted the description of the same one that was found, around an hour later.

The apron wasn't there previously, we know that it was there for only a short time, just less than 50 minutes, according to the timing of the police officer's beats. It seems more likely that when we think of it like this, the likelihood of this apron being Catherine Eddowes increases. Especially when we take all of these points into account.

It could have been animal blood, but, there's no reason to assume that is was. Given that the apron was found between 2.20am and 2.55am, it probably would have been the quietest time, where hardly anyone was about. That makes the odds of this being the apron of Catherine Eddowes, even greater. What's the odds that someone else left a blood-stained apron there within that hour? Probably little.

We can't say with certainty that this was the apron of Catherine Eddowes, given that we can't test the apron today, as it has been destroyed. But, given the probability, it seems highly likely, for the reasons stated, that this apron, was the apron of Catherine Eddowes. And therefore, a physical piece of evidence left behind by Jack the Ripper.

It is the only physical piece of evidence that Jack the Ripper left. Unless of course he was also responsible for the Goulston Street graffiti. The Goulston Street graffiti was found on a wall above where the apron was found.[lxxxix]

The graffiti read:

"The Juwes are the men that shall not be blamed for nothing"[xc]

It's a statement that can be open to interpretation. It is a statement which is specific, but not specific enough. It seems that whoever wrote this, was trying to say that Jewish people are being targeted unfairly. Which we know, is true.

During the Whitechapel Murders, there was an anti-Semitic feeling in the area. There were high levels of immigration from European countries and, people within Whitechapel became highly resentful of the immigrants that were settling in Whitechapel. Many of these immigrants were Jews.[xci] This anti-Semitic feeling within Whitechapel at the time was so strong, that riots occurred towards the Jewish community.[xcii]

The riots were not only down to people feeling resentful towards the Jewish community. They were also feeling resentful towards the police for not catching the killer – Jack the Ripper. They were also feeling angry that the killer had not been caught.

The fact that the police had not caught the killer, resulted in the residents of Whitechapel taking matters into their own hands. Were they would patrol the streets in search for the killer and groups such as the Whitechapel Vigilance Committee set being up for members of the public to patrol the streets.[xciii]

We know today that the establishment of the Whitechapel Vigilance Committee and the extra patrols on the streets, both by ordinary members of the public and by those who were in the police, resulted in nothing. It did not result in the killer being caught and it didn't really result in anything much.

The only thing that perhaps it could reveal, is what we learn from the From Hell letter. We will get to that later on in the book. But now, we are going to round up on Catherine Eddowes and move onto Jack the Ripper's final victim, Mary Jane Kelly.

In hindsight when we look at the Double Event night, it looks as if Jack the Ripper should have been caught that night. How he wasn't caught that night is a mystery. Was he just extremely lucky in evading the police and public from capture? Was he calculated and knew the routes of the police? With Catherine Eddowes only being arrested late on the night of the 29th of September 1888, it seems that if Jack was just extremely lucky.

He couldn't have possibly know poor Catherine was being released that night. It seems just unfortunate timing on Catherine's part that she was at the wrong place, at the wrong time. Although, if Jack the Ripper was a police officer, then, he could have possibly known that Catherine was being released that night.

If Jack was a police officer, which some have speculated that he was, he would have had a good idea about police patrols too. With the events of the Double Event, it shows that either Jack the Ripper was sporadic, opportunistic, out of control and extreme lucky in getting away that night. Not once, but twice. Or, he was a police officer.

If he was a police officer, he would have knew exactly what he was doing, knew how to evade the police because he would have had a good knowledge of their beats. And, knew that Catherine would be released that night and so knew she would have been an easy target. Perhaps the attack in Mitre Square wasn't as risky as it seems, if you were a police officer knowing the timings, it probably be safer than any other place.

Not many members of the public wander about the headquarters of police stations. When it comes to these two theories, I don't know, at this moment what theory I prefer. So, I'm not ruling one out over the other. When it comes to the Jack the Ripper case, I remain open minded as I think most of the theories are speculative and circumstantial.

Mary Jane Kelly

The final Jack the Ripper victim of the Canonical Five, was, Mary Jane Kelly.[xciv] Although it is contested whether Mary Jane Kelly was actually the final Jack the Ripper victim, as there are arguments from some Ripperologists that she was not the final Jack the Ripper victim. It's more likely that she was a victim of the ripper, than not. Therefore, we are going to conclude that she was the final Jack the Ripper victim.

Mary Jane Kelly was the final Canonical Five victim who was murdered in the early morning hours of the 9th of November 1888. Unlike the other Jack the Ripper victims, Mary Jane Kelly was not murdered outside on the streets of Whitechapel. Instead, Mary

Jane Kelly was murdered indoors, where she lived, which makes her murder slightly different.

Before we get to the actual murder of Mary Jane Kelly, let us look at her final hours and see what happened in her life. The final hours of Mary Jane Kelly's life, aren't as well documented as some of the other Canonical Five victims, especially when it comes to the night, not the early morning hours, the details of Mary Jane Kelly's life are not as well known. Perhaps part of the reason for not knowing much about her, was because she was so much younger than the other Jack the Ripper victims.

Let's document what we do know about her final hours. What we do know is that nothing throughout the day of her final hours, is much known, on the 8th of November 1888. We know that some-time between 7pm and 8pm, Joseph Barnett, a love interest of Mary Jane Kelly's, visited her between that time. Mary was home at 13 Miller's Court with.[xcv]some women.

It's thought that 13 Miller's Court where Mary Jane Kelly lived, was perhaps a brothel. The influx and outflux of women into 13 Miller's Court, suggests that she could have been using Miller's Court as a brothel. Though, we can't say this with certain. What further suggest Miller's Court being used as a brothel, is that when Mary Jane Kelly's body was found on the morning of the 9th of November 1888[xcvi] This suggest that either she let the ripper inside, or perhaps the ripper knew her, as there was no forced entry into 13 Miller's Court. The ripper didn't appear to break entry into the house.

This give us an insight into how Jack might have lured his victims. It suggests that perhaps Jack the Ripper posed as a client before he murdered the women. That would explain why there was no forced entry. However, with the way Mary's clothes were found the following morning, it indicates that there could have been another reason. Mary's clothes were found folded up, she was wearing a dressing gown, which indicates either she was getting ready to go in bed or was already in bed.

Perhaps Mary Jane Kelly knew her killer and she let him in. Either way, it appears that Mary Jane Kelly may have let Jack the Ripper in willingly that night. Either that, or her door was left open (but it wasn't open the following morning).

Back to that evening. Barnett didn't stay at Miller's Court that evening, he left sometime between 7pm and 8pm that evening.[xcvii] Barnet left with a friend of Mary's who lived at Miller's Court, Maria. Therefore, it's apparent that Barnett did not stay long. It's not really clear why Joseph Barnet was at Miller's Court. Though, he was an on-off love interest of Mary Jane Kelly's.

From this, we can gather that Mary Jane Kelly and Joseph Barnett had a good relationship after they parted. At least, it appears that they kept on friendly terms. The problem with Mary Jane Kelly though, and Joseph Barnett's interpretation of events, is that everything that we know about Mary Jane Kelly, rests on what we are told by Joseph Barnett about her.[xcviii]

Therefore, if we are to believe everything that we know about

Mary Jane Kelly, then, we must believe Joseph Barnett and he must be telling the truth. The truth about Mary Jane Kelly, rests on the assumption that Joseph Barnett is not lying. The problem is, is that we don't really have any other sources about Mary Jane Kelly. Which is problematic.

The identity of Mary Jane Kelly can't really be confirmed, as her DNA has not been proven.[xcix] Mary Jane Kelly is the most mysterious suspect of all of them.

When he left Miller's Court, he went back to the residence he was staying at. That residency was Buller's Boarding House. He stayed there all night and went to bed at 12.30am. It would give Joseph Barnett a strong alibi, one which means that he probably didn't murder Mary Jane; neither was he Jack the Ripper. This is important to point out, as Joseph Barnett has been accused of being Jack the Ripper and is a ripper suspect.

Some would say, but he could have sneaked out during the night. True. However, there is no evidence that he did sneak out. No one saw him doing so. He lived in a house which was full of people, it probably would have been difficult for him to go out unnoticed. So, it's more than likely that he did not go out that evening. He has a strong alibi, he was playing cards that night at his residence and went to bed at 12.30am, with no sighting of him going out afterwards.

The next few hours is unknown when it comes to Mary Jane Kelly, she must have went out sometime between 8pm and 11.45pm that evening, as we know that she went out, due to someone seeing her return to her home. She came back that night to 13 Miller's Court with a man at 11.45pm, as seen by a fellow prostitute, Mary Anne Cox.[c]

It's possible that Mary was out soliciting for trade during those hours or she was in the Ten Bells. The Ten Bells is a pub in Whitechapel which every Jack the Ripper victim went to. Most likely she was for soliciting for trade before she returned to Miller's Court, as she returned to Miller's Court with a man.[ci]

We know that she returned to Miller's Court at this time because of Mary Ann Cox, who saw her with the man. Mary Ann Cox had a brief exchanging of words with Mary Jane Kelly. What we do know from Mary Ann Cox, is that Mary Jane Kelly was drunk when Mary Ann Cox saw her. Which is why it was most likely that she was in the Ten Bells previously. Or, she was drinking somewhere else.

The pair didn't talk for long. The brief exchange of words they had were:

"Goodnight" said Mary Ann Cox

"Goodnight, I am going to sing." replied Mary Jane.[cii]

A few moments later, Mary Jane Kelly did indeed start to sing. She started to sing A Violet From A Mother's Grave, which seems a bit eerily fitting with what was about to happen to poor Mary. Singing at night must have been something that Mary Jane Kelly did frequently, as she sang a few times throughout that night, just before her gruesome murder. Also, Mary Cox didn't seem surprised that she was going to sing.

Mary Jane Kelly seems to have been signing for at least 45 minutes, as when Mary Ann Cox was going back out at 12.30am, she still heard Mary Jane Kelly singing. It's possible that she could have been signing on and off, rather than through the entirety of the 45 minutes. Before Mary Ann Cox left to go out, her husband was about to go and complain[ciii] about Mary Jane Kelly's singing.

Then Mrs Cox replied to him, *"You leave that poor woman alone!"* Either Mary's signing was quite loud, or, the houses were so close together. By the photographs of the area, it looks as if the houses were very close together.

Mrs Cox returned only a half an hour later, to find that Mary Jane Kelly was still singing and that her room light was on. By a half an hour later, Mary Jane Kelly had stopped singing, according to another neighbour, Elizabeth Prater.[civ] Mrs Prater was out that night, before she returned home, she stood outside Miller's Court talking to John McCarthy,[cv] but she didn't see anyone go in at that time.

At some point, Mary Jane Kelly left Miller's Court again, but exactly at what time, we don't know. It's most likely that she went back out after 1.30am that morning, on the morning of the 9th of November 1888. But, it could have been later than that. Most likely it was around sometime at about 1.55am that she left Miller's Court, because a man called George Hutchinson saw her at

2am on Commercial Street.[cvi]

By looking at the map of Whitechapel, we can see that Miller's Court and Commercial Street are right next to one another, which means that it couldn't have take Mary Jane Kelly longer than five minutes to walk from Miller's Court to Commercial Street. So, that's why she probably left around 1.55am from Miller's Court. But, that's just speculative.

There is no eye witness of seeing her leave Miller's Court.

When George Hutchinson met Mary Jane Kelly on Commercial Street on the morning of the 9th of November 1888, he said that she asked him for a sixpence. She asked him, *"Mr. Hutchinson, can you lend me sixpence?",* to which he replied, *'I can't."* Before she walked off towards Thrawl Street, Mary Jane Kelly finished by saying, *"I spent all my money going down to Romford. Good morning, I must go and find some money."*[cvii]

It might seem strange that she was out looking for money that morning, given that she actually had a house, unlike the other four women Jack the Ripper killed. The other Jack the Ripper victims lived in dose houses. But, from what happened later that morning, it's clear that she was overdue on rent money, so, it's possible that that is why she was out on the street that morning – if not it being the most likely reason.

As Mary Jane Kelly walked away from Hutchinson, another man greeted Mary. She said to him, *"Alright".* To which this man replied, *"You will be alright for what I have told you."*[cviii] It's not really known what he meant by this statement.

The interesting thing about this man, is that he was carrying a parcel. It might not seem relevant or interesting on the surface that this man was carrying a parcel. However, think back to when we were discussing Elizabeth Stride's murder, and the pipe man with the parcel when she was murdered, it becomes more interesting then.

Why would someone need a parcel at those times of the morning? Could Jack the Ripper have hid his knife, or knifes, in a parcel? It's possible, since we don't actually know what he was carrying on those nights, since we don't know who he was. Of course, the parcel thing could be just grasping at straws. However, we should be looking for similarities that show up with people who are seen with the murder victims.

If we see similarities, then, perhaps it indicates that they are the same person. But that's just speculation, it would be impossible to tell. Hutchinson saw the man and Mary Jane Kelly head off towards Commercial Street. Then down towards Dorset Street. Hutchinson hears Mary Jane Kelly say to the *man "All right, my dear. Come along. You will be comfortable."*[cix] This is the last time that Mary Jane Kelly was probably seen alive.

We say probably, because there was thought to have been a sighting of Mary Jane Kelly at 8.30am that morning, by a woman called Caroline Maxwell.[cx] This sighting was probably someone else that Maxwell saw. We can make this assumptions for two reasons. The first, is that Jack the Ripper didn't kill during daylight hours.

He had a pattern of killing in the early morning hours. Secondly, the doctor who examined Mary Jane Kelly, estimated that the time of death was a few hours before Maxwell's sighting.

This means, that Hutchinson and the man Mary Jane Kelly was with, were likely the last two people to see her alive, besides Mary Jane Kelly's killer – Jack the Ripper. Though, it's led to Hutchinson and the unknown man being classed as Jack the Ripper suspects.

Whether Hutchinson was Jack the Ripper, is a debate in itself. But, according to him, he left where he was standing watching Mary Jane Kelly's door until 3am that morning. Then, according to him, he left at around that time. Hutchinson may not have been Jack the Ripper, but, he was acting odd and stalker-like. So, it's not like Hutchinson was acting in a way which was healthy. His behaviour indicates that he may have had an obsession with Mary Jane Kelly.

Either way, he saw no one leave the house during the time he stood there. This indicates one or two things. Either, the man Mary Jane Kelly went into her house with, was Jack the Ripper. Or, the man left sometime after Hutchinson left and then Jack the Ripper entered the house.

It's uncertain which. However, Jack the Ripper probably entered after, this man had left. Why? Well, it seems Mary Jane Kelly was probably alive for at least another hour. There's plenty of time for the man to have left and then afterwards, Jack the Ripper had entered.

We know Mary Jane must have been alive at this time, because according to Mrs Cox, Mary Jane Kelly's neighbour, heard men coming in and out of Miller's Court throughout the early morning hours. However, she did say she was coming home at 3am and didn't see a light or hear any sound from Mary Jane Kelly's room.[cxi]

This would support what was going on in the room, the way it was left. Mary Jane Kelly's room looked as if she went to bed. With her clothes folded and her boots at the fireplace. Therefore, if she did settle down for the night, it leads us to ask about the entrance of Jack the Ripper into the house.

It doesn't appear as if there was a forced entry by Jack the Ripper with Miller's Court. Therefore, either the door was open or Mary Jane Kelly let her killer in. The latter is very important, because, if she did let her killer in, then that perhaps suggests she knew her killer. We can't say this with certainty though, and it is an assumption.

However, it appears as if she went out in search for clients, then brought them back to her house. Which indicates that she didn't just tell clients to come home. Although, it's speculation. If she had gone to sleep, it means that she must have been finished work for the night. Which also means, that whoever showed up at her home, wasn't expected.

Jack the Ripper wasn't expected.

Whether Mary Jane Kelly knew her killer is open to speculation. But, given that there was no sigh of a forced entry and, no cry of help when the killer made his way in. Lastly, Mary Jane Kelly could have left the door open for some reason and went to bed. As her body was found on the bed, it's possible she was sleeping when she was attacked.

What we do know, is that around 4am, Miss Kelly's neighbour, Elizabeth Prater, hears a cry of *"Oh murder"*, as she woke up because her pet cat Diddles woke her up.[cxii] Another neighbour, Sarah Lewis, also hears the cry. Neither make nothing of it and don't go to inspect it, as such cries were common at the time. Could this have been the moment that Mary Jane Kelly was murdered?

It's possible.

What we do know is that it would fit with Mary Jane Kelly's assumed time of death. An interesting dissertation, called 'Estimating Mary Kelly's time of death'.[cxiii] It estimates the time of Mary Jane Kelly's murder as some time between 3am and 4am that morning. Given that Jack the Ripper murdered his other victims at roughly the same time, alongside the reports of Hutchinson leaving and the neighbours hearing the cries of *'Oh murder!'*, I'm inclined to agree.

According to the dissertation also, the ripper would have attacked and mutilated Mary within 30 minutes. I would agree with that too, given the timings of the other murders. This would mean that it is unlikely that the man Hutchinson seen with Mary, couldn't have been the killer. The killer must have entered Miller's Court, shortly after the man left.

The body of Mary Jane Kelly was found a few hours later that morning, by a man called John McCarthy at 10.45am.[cxiv] John McCarthy was there to collect overdue rent from Mary Jane Kelly, what he found was her mutilated body by looking through the window. The door could not be open. The door had to be broken into by the police a few hours later.

The murder of Mary Jane Kelly was by far the most horrible of the Jack the Ripper murders. He mutilated Mary Jane beyond any recognition. Some have even theorized that this was Jack the Ripper's ultimate sick fantasy – what he was aiming for. He certainly had more time with Miss Kelly, than the other victims, because he killed her indoors. Whereas, the other victims were killed outside and he had to flee more quickly.

What is noticeable with the Canonical Five victims, is that there was a progression of ghastliness with the murders. As each murder occurred, it became more ghastly than the last one. This has led Jack the Ripper to become a notorious figure in history, while also installing fear into the residents of Whitechapel during the Autumn of 1888.

The Canonical Five victims are the victims which most experts agree with who Jack the Ripper killed. However, it's also been thought that Jack the Ripper also had other victims. This is what we are going to explore in the next chapter – the other potential

Jennifer Helen Johnstone

victims of Jack the Ripper.

CHAPTER THREE: THE OTHER POTENTIAL JACK THE RIPPER VICTIMS

There are other potential victims of Jack the Ripper. These victims are known as the Whitechapel Murder victims.[cxv] The Whitechapel Murder victims are known as the Whitechapel Murders. The Whitechapel Murders included eleven women who were murdered and included in the Whitechapel Murder File.[cxvi] Since these murders occurred, it has been debated whether Jack the Ripper committed the murders.

At one point or another, all these eleven victims were thought to have been killed by Jack the Ripper. There is still a debate about whether they were victims of Jack the Ripper. You've already looked at most of these victims, Emma Smith, Martha Tabram, Mary Ann Nichols, Annie Chapman, Elizabeth Stride, Catherine Eddowes and Mary Jane Kelly. In this chapter, we are going to look at the other four victims.

The Whitechapel Murders occurred from April 1888 up until February 1891.[cxvii] They include a total of 11 victims, all of them women and all most likely to have been prostitutes, who were murdered in the Whitechapel district. They have all thought to have been killed by Jack the Ripper, at one point or another. However, today, it is thought that most of these women were not murdered by Jack.

Those not murdered by Jack, were those not included in the Canonical Five. Let's look at those women who are part of the Whitechapel Murders, but are not thought to have been ripper victims. We shall look at these victims in chronological order. The first Whitechapel Murder victim, was called Emma Smith, who was murdered on the 3rd of April 1888.[cxviii] Emma died on the 4th, just a day later. She lived long enough to describe her attack. It's clear that Emma wasn't murdered by Jack the Ripper, because she was robbed and murdered by a gang.

In this respect, her murder is vastly different from the Canonical Five victims. Therefore, she was not a Jack the Ripper victim. The same assumption cannot be said for the next Whitechapel Murder victim; Martha Tabram.

Martha Tabram was the second Whitechapel Murder victim, who was murdered on the 7th of August 1888.[cxix] Martha seems to be the most controversial Whitechapel Murder victim, because many people seem to think that Martha Tabram was the first Jack the Ripper victim.[cxx] There are several good reasons why Martha Tabram could have been a victim of Jack the Ripper.

Like the Canonical Five victims, Martha was a middle-aged prostitute that was murdered in the early morning hours. However, unlike the Canonical Five victims, it appears Martha was stabbed multiple times, whereas, the Canonical victims had their throats slit, while being mutilated. This is why some people think that Martha's murder was different. However, there are similarities with Martha's death, and the five.

Given the other similarities, such as being a middle-aged prostitute, murdered in the early morning hours in Whitechapel, at roughly the same time as the Canonical

victims, it's led others to believe that Martha was in fact the first Jack the Ripper victim.

In truth, we will probably never know whether Martha was a victim of Jack's.

We can't say for certain. However, given that she has many similarities with the other victims, there seems to be a good chance, unfortunately, that she was a victim of Jack's. She is the most likely out of the others.

Let's look at some of the facts surrounding the murder of Martha Tabram:

. Prostitute
. Drinking problem
. Relationship/marriage problems
. Murder between 2am and 3.30am

We know her murder was between this time, because of witness testimonies. Two residents of George We know her murder was between this time, because of witness testimonies. Two residents of George Yard Buildings, Elizabeth and Joseph Mahoney, were entering George Yard Buildings at 2am. They didn't see anything unusual.

This means, that Martha must have been alive by this point, because her body wasn't there. Martha was last seen alive by George Yard Buildings by Mary Ann Connelly at 11.45pm on the 6th of August 1888,[cxxi] they were with two soldiers, who were clients of the women. The women parted ways with a solider each at that time, with Martha going into George Yard.

This had led to speculation that the woman that Martha went off with, was her killer. However, this raises some questions. They could have been in the yard for up to four and a half hours, if this is true, then why did they wait around the yard all that time? And why did no one see them? Yes, it was early in the morning, but, the two residents that appeared in the yard at 2am, didn't see anyone. They also didn't report anything that was out of the ordinary.

There was also a PC, called PC Thomas Barrett, who was patrolling the area, he didn't see anything while he was patrolling the area. Then, at 3.30am, Albert George Crow was returning home to enter George Yard Buildings after a night out working, he saw the body of Martha Tabram lying at the bottom of the stairs. However, he didn't think anything of it, she thought she was just sleeping.[cxxii]

He thought this because it was pitch black and there were no lights there. Therefore, he didn't realize that she was dead. It wasn't until an hour and a half later, at 5am, that Martha's body was really discovered, by George Yard resident, John Saunders Reeves, who was on his way to work that morning.[5] Just a half an hour later, doctor Timothy Killeen arrived on the scene at 5.30am and pronounced that Martha had been dead for 3 hours.[cxxiii]

If Doctor Killeen is correct, then Martha must have been murdered at around 2.30am. Which puts her death in the time frame we were saying, a time frame between 2am and 3.30am. Which means that the time from when she was last seen at 11.45pm and 3.30am when she was found, means that there is a gap of almost 3 hours.

It would require an explanation of where she was for 3 hours and more importantly, who she was with. It's possible that she could have spent all that time with the solider. Or, she could have come across another person who killed her.

Either way, we will likely never know. But, if we treat Martha Tabram as Jack the Ripper's first victim, then, he could have been a solider, or, he could have lived somewhere near the proximity of George Yard Buildings. It seems like too much of a coincidence that poor Martha shared many similarities with Jack's other victims to rule her out as a victim of Jack the Ripper.

Martha was the last Whitechapel Murder victim before the Canonical Five murders began. The Canonical Five Murders began just a few weeks later at the end of August that same month, with the murder of Mary Ann Nichols. Then, in September 1888, there was a total of three murders. First there was Annie Chapman, who was murdered just over a week after Mary Ann Nichols.

Then, two murders happened at the end of September. The first woman was Elizabeth Stride and the second woman was Catherine Eddowes. There were no murders which happened in October, that we know about. Then, what many believe to be Jack the Ripper's last murder occurred at the start of November, with that of Mary Jane Kelly.

However, the Whitechapel murder file was not closed there. There were several other murders (or suspicious deaths), which were recorded on the Whitechapel Murder file. These murders don't really get that much attention, as today, it's not thought that they were committed by Jack.

The eight women on the Whitechapel Murders file, was a woman called Rose Mylett. Rose Mylett was a prostitute, who also had a drinking problem, who was murdered (but some have speculated suicide), in the early morning hours of the 20th of December 1888. Her murder occurred in the Whitechapel area, just a few weeks after the murder of Mary Jane Kelly. It's for these reasons, that Rose Mylett was on the Whitechapel Murder file. Today, however, she is not thought to have been a victim of Jack the Ripper.

Why?

If Rose was murdered, then she would have been murdered by being strangled, according to the post-mortem report.[cxxiv] If she was, then it would make the modus operandi different from that of that used by Jack the Ripper. This would mean that if someone did murder Rose Mylett, she most likely had a different murder. And therefore, her murderer couldn't have been Jack the Ripper.

However, her death may not have been a murder. There are conflicting reports from the time. Others involved in the case thought that Rose Mylett's death wasn't a murder, as there were no signs of struggle at the time of death.[cxxv] Which has led to the theory that she either killed herself, or that her death was an accident. Her death likely wasn't linked to the ripper murders.

This was the last incident of 1888, it wasn't until the following year, on the 17th of July 1889.[cxxvi] This is when the murder of Frances Cole took place. The murder of Frances Cole took place at around midnight, she was also found mutilated. This led to the police at the time suspecting Frances to be a victim of Jack's.

Her murder was most likely that of a copycat killer, rather than being that of Jack the Ripper. Which means, that she most likely wasn't a victim of Jack's. Frances Cole was the tenth woman fund in the Whitechapel Murders. Her body was the last of the Whitechapel Murder victims found, which drew a close to the case in 1891.

The eleventh and final Jack the Ripper victim found, was that of an unidentified woman. It was only her torso that was found.

So, who this belonged to, is a mystery. The Whitechapel Murders closed after this discovery, in 1891.

To this day, there has been no identification of Jack the Ripper and much of what happened in the Whitechapel Murders, remains a mystery to this day.

The Whitechapel Murders raise many questions. These include 'Why did the killings start?' 'What was their motivation?' 'Why did they stop?' and 'What made them stop?' 'What happened to Jack the Ripper?' and of course, 'Who was Jack the Ripper?' All these things remain unanswered to this day. Though, there are different theories to these questions, depending on who you ask.

We are now going to go onto chapter four, where we are going to look at what Whitechapel was like in 1888.

CHAPTER FOUR: WHITECHAPEL LONDON IN 1888

Whitechapel had many problems within in during 1888, the Whitechapel area was a slum during the Victorian era, including in 1888.[cxxvii] It was a slum area which was riddle with crime, poverty, homelessness and prostitution. Women were forced into prostitution, due to things such as there not being enough or any work for women.[cxxviii]

Jack the Ripper's victims, were forced into prostitution through a break down in marriage. Then, with there no jobs for them, and no men to support them, women were forced into that prostitution.

This led to a cycle of thousands of women in the Whitechapel area, not having a stable home. They didn't have a home, they rented a bed every night – which highlights the extent of poverty within the Whitechapel area of the time.

Whitechapel in 1888, wasn't a pleasant place to live. It was a place riddled with crime, prostitution, ill-health, overcrowding, poverty and, for what 1888 was most infamous for – murder.[cxxix] In many ways, Whitechapel was a forgotten area. Forgotten by the establishment and well-off.

That was until the Jack the Ripper events. Jack the Ripper forced the establishment and the rich of the country, to pay attention to the Whitechapel area. But it went further than that, it forced the World's attention to be shone on the Whitechapel area. With media attention drawn to the most impoverished area of London.[cxxx] Media outlets from all over the World reported on the Jack the Ripper crimes.[cxxxi]

The ghastly nature of the crimes were one reason why the media was drawn to these murders. Another reason was the impoverished nature of these murders. No one could further ignore Whitechapel or its people. Whitechapel at the time of 1888, made a Dickens novel look glamorised in comparison.

Charles Dickens done a great job of highlighting the impoverished nature of poor Victorians. He done an excellent job of showing the World how poor Victorians were treated and what their situations were like. However, his works didn't highlight the true extent to the deprivation and awful conditions that poor Victorians lived in.

The Whitechapel murders done that. If it wasn't for the Whitechapel murders, then perhaps the true extent of Victorian poverty and deprivation, might not be know today. However, there is evidence that there were changing attitudes towards the poor before 1888. Through things such as Charles Dickens work, such as Oliver Twist.[cxxxii]

However, Charles Dickens fictional tales may have been influential, but only to an extent. His later work, A Christmas Carol (1848) highlighted how the poor were forgotten, looked down upon and exploited by the rich.[cxxxiii] Although Dicken's novel is fiction, his retelling of Victorian attitudes towards the poor aren't. This is further highlighted in how people in Whitechapel were treated by their richer counterparts.

We see with Jack the Ripper's victims, that they are not given any consideration. Their well-being isn't considered. We see the women who were murdered being forced out onto the streets to collect money. These streets were knowingly dangerous by the men who forced them out onto the streets. Yet, there wasn't a consideration for the woman's safety. This kind of attitude is resonated in the works of Charles Dickens.

It is things like this, that show us Victorian attitudes towards the poor. Or, more specifically, the attitude of richer Victorians towards the poorer Victorians. Therefore, we can gather that Victorian Whitechapel in 1888, was a heartless society.

However, a lack of education and a lack of jobs for the citizens of Whitechapel, also played a part in Whitechapel conditions. In the Victorian era, most children did not go to school. It was not mandatory for most children to go to school for most of the Victorian era.

That changed in 1870, when it became mandatory for children between 5 years old and 10 years old to go to school.[cxxxiv] This changed in 1893, when it became mandatory for children up to 11 years old to go to school.[cxxxv] This meant that at the time of Jack the Ripper, children were only

required to go to school for five years. While they were teenagers, it was not mandatory for children to go to school. Therefore, children didn't get a lengthy and good education and, they ended up working while they were still children.

There's evidence to show that poverty and a lack of education is interlinked. Therefore, if there was a lack of education in Whitechapel residents, then it resulted in poverty in later life.[cxxxvi] Poorer Victorians also would have done less well in school and would have went to work while they were still children, in order to help their families who were in poverty.

In other words, it became a cycle for people who were born into poverty in the Victorian era. Those Victorians born in poverty, had their odds stacked against them. If they were born into poverty, they were likely to die in poverty. Their poverty was a result of a lack of education, the way society was structured and a lack of jobs.

In many ways, this was worse if you were a woman in Victorian Whitechapel. Victorian woman weren't seen as equal to men, they were seen as secondary citizens. Therefore, if they were not supported by men, then they would find themselves in determinantal conditions. Which is exactly what happened to all of Jack the Ripper's victims, perhaps with an exemption of Mary Jane Kelly, as she was young and unmarried.

But, for the other victims, when their marriages broke down and they did not have a husband to support them, is when their problems really kicked in.

So, what was Whitechapel like at the time of Jack the Ripper? If you could think of a Charles Dickens novel such as Oliver Twist, then imagine an adult version of that, then, that is what Whitechapel at the time of Jack the Ripper was like.

The letters of the Jack the Ripper case highlighted how dark Whitechapel was at the time of the ripper killing. In the next chapter, we are going to look at the most infamous letters in the Jack the Ripper case.

CHAPTER FIVE: THE LETTERS OF JACK THE RIPPER

Throughout the Jack the Ripper events, there were hundreds of letters which were sent to the police.[cxxxvii] It is thought that the vast majority of these letters were a hoax. I agree. However, there is one letter that stands out from all the other letters. That letter is the From Hell letter.[cxxxviii] There is good reason to suspect that the From Hell letter was an authentic letter.

The main reason that this letter was probably sent by Jack the Ripper, was the fact that it was sent with half a human kidney.[cxxxix] This suggests that the letter is more than just a hoax. It's one thing to write a letter, pretending that you are Jack the Ripper. It's quite another thing to send half a human kidney with a forged letter – that goes further.

There are other reasons to suggest that the From Hell letter was authentic. Unlike the other Jack the Ripper letters, the From Hell letter wasn't sent to the police, it was sent to a man called George Lusk.[cxl] George Lusk was an ordinary member of the public, who set up a group called The Whitechapel Vigilance Committee.[cxli] What does this tell us?

Well, if the letter was sent by Jack the Ripper, then, it tells us two things about Jack the Ripper. It tells us that a) He was a local who was well aware that there were groups of people outside the police trying to catch the killer. And b) that Jack the Ripper knew Mr Lusk personally. Not just because he addresses Mr Lusk, but also because he sounds as if he is familiar with him.

It raises an interesting question, could Jack the Ripper went so far as to go on the Whitechapel Vigilance Committee? If he was on the Whitechapel Vigilance Committee, then he would have making himself appear as if he was working to catch the killer, rather than be the killer.

Let's say that Jack the Ripper isn't on the list of suspects, and we are looking for someone, a suspect, which isn't on the suspect list, let's look at who was part of the committee. According to the British Library, the committee was largely made up of shop keepers and business owners.[cxlii] If Jack was on the committee, then could he have been a shop keeper or business owner? It's possible, nothing can be ruled out when it comes to Jack the Ripper.

This is what the From Hell letter actually said:

'From hell

Mr Lusk,
Sor
I send you half the Kidne I took from one woman and prasarved it for
you tother piece I fried and ate it was very nise. I may send you the
bloody knif that took it out if you only wate a whil longer
signed
Catch me when you can Mishter Lusk.[cxliii]

The letter isn't that long and doesn't appear to be well written,
you can see from the picture below.

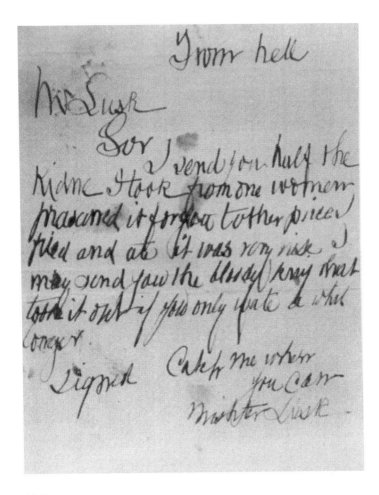

There are a few things that are apparent from this letter. The first thing that is apparent, is that it is directly addressed to George Lusk, so it's personal. He knows Mr Lusk. This is also apparent from the fact that this letter was sent to George Lusk's home, at Alderney Street on the 16th of the 16th of October 1888.[cxliv]

This is different from the other letters, which were sent to the police and London's Central news Agency. The From Hell letter along with the half kidney was sent to Mr Lusk's home at 5pm that day.[cxlv] George also had a stalker following him or several days before that.[cxlvi]

Could this have been the same man that delivered the From Hell letter? It's possible that it was. We can't say for certain. What we can say, is that it's perhaps too much of a coincidence. It's possible that the same man was Jack the Ripper.

The From Hell letter is the most interesting Jack the Ripper letter. There are several reasons for this. This includes: for its content, the mysterious stalker man, it being sent to Mr Lusk on what seems like a personal level, and of course, the gruesome half a human kidney that was sent along with it. But it wasn't the only letter.

There are a few other infamous letters which were sent to the police. These letters don't appear to be authentic. With one journalist even claiming that he wrote one of the letters. That letter, was the Dear Boss letter.[cxlvii] The Dear Boss letter is as significant as the From Hell letter. The From Hell letter is significant because, if it was sent from Jack the Ripper, then it gives us a lot more clues to his identity.

The Dear Boss letter is significant for another reason. It's significant because it gave birth to the name 'Jack the Ripper.' The Dear Boss letter is how Jack the Ripper got his name.[cxlviii] Before the Dear Boss letter was sent on the 27th of September 1888, Jack the Ripper was known as the Whitechapel Murderer, or Leather Apron. He wasn't known as Jack the Ripper until after the Double Event, when the letter was published.

If the Dear Boss letter wasn't created, then we wouldn't have the name, Jack the Ripper to describe him. If it wasn't for the name, perhaps Jack the Ripper, wouldn't be as infamous today, as he now is. Leather Apron or the Whitechapel Murderer, the names that he was known as beforehand, doesn't have the same ring to it as Jack the Ripper – it doesn't have the same fear factor.

The content of the letter is less well known as the name it provided. Here is what the Dear Boss letter actually said:

'Dear Boss,

I keep on hearing the police have caught me. but they wont fix me just yet. I have laughed when they look so clever and talk about being on the right track. That joke about Leather Apron gave me real fits.
I am down on whores and I shant quit ripping them till I do get buckled. Grand work the last job was. I gave the lady no time to squeal. How can they catch me now. I love my work and want to start again. You will

soon hear of me with my funny little games.

I saved some of the proper red stuff in a ginger beer bottle over the last job to write with but it went thick like glue and I cant use it. Red ink is fit enough I hope ha. ha. The next job I do I shall clip the ladys ears off and send to the police officers just for jolly wouldn't you.

Keep this letter back till I do a bit more work. then give it out straight. My knife's so nice and sharp I want to get to work right away if I get a chance. Good luck.

Yours truly
Jack the Ripper
Dont mind me giving the trade name
Wasnt good enough to post this before I got all the red ink off my hands curse it No luck yet. They say I'm a doctor now- ha ha'.[cxlix]

This is probably a hoax, like the other ripper letters. It has a different style of writing than the From Hell letter, which suggests that they are from two different authors. A new study of this letter (and the Saucy Jack Postcard) has confirmed that the two letters were written that they were written by the same hand. The same study also found that these two letters were a hoax, to boost business journalists.[cl]

In other words, journalists forged both the Dear Boss letter, and the Saucy Jack Postcard, to boost newspaper sales at the time of the murders.

The next infamous Jack the Ripper letter, is known as the Saucy Jack Postcard. The Saucy Jack Postcard is another short letter. It reads:

> "I was not codding dear old Boss when I gave you the tip, you'll hear about Saucy Jacky's work tomorrow double event this time number one squealed a bit couldn't finish straight off. ha not the time to get ears for police. thanks for keeping last letter back till I got to work again.

Jack the Ripper"[cli]

The postcard was sent just after the Double Event, on the next day. This would have given the hoaxer enough time to hoax the letter. Others disagree, some believe that the postcard is genuine. Though, this has been disproven by modern research.

These are the most infamous letters associated with the Jack the Ripper case. They were sent during September 1888 and October 1888. Notably, there were no killings by Jack the Ripper during October 1888, that we know about.

That was probably down to the Double Event. He almost got caught that night. Perhaps that forced him to lay low. Though, if the From Hell letter was from Jack, the he was taunting and trying to in-store fear again by mid-October.

There were hundreds of letters sent to the police claiming to be from Jack the Ripper in late 1888. Most of these letters at the time, were thought to have been hoaxes by the public. The only three letters that were taken seriously, were the three letters named in this chapter: the From Hell letter, the Dear Boss letter, and the Saucy Jack Postcard.

Now that you have had an introduction to the case, let's go on to the second part of the book. The second part of the book is going to look at the suspects and evidence.

CHAPTER SIX: THE JACK THE RIPPER SUSPECTS

T he most interesting part of the Jack the Ripper case, is in trying to solve who Jack the Ripper was. This case has been a mystery for historians and Ripperologists for almost 130 years now. There have been many theories presented as to who Jack the Ripper was. But, has anyone successfully proved who Jack the Ripper was?

Sometimes with the case, it feels as if people are trying to fit their chosen suspect into the facts, rather than fitting the facts towards a suspect. In other words, it can feel like there is a need for some Ripperologists to convince us of their candidate. Rather than looking at the facts and then trying to see who is most likely suspect to be the ripper.

This chapter isn't going to convince you of who Jack the Ripper was. This chapter is instead going to look at some of the suspects.

The suspects we're going to focus on, are suspects which seem more credible than others. Although, even with the best suspects, the evidence is thin and non-existent. It's really based on character, timing and police insight (who they thought the killer was).

There is no real physical evidence we have on the case. Which makes it difficult, if not impossible, to name who Jack the Ripper was. With every suspect, it seems as if all of them are suspected on circumstantial evidence, rather than any physical evidence, proving that they were the killer.

Here are few Jack the Ripper suspects who have been suspected of being Jack the Ripper over the years. None of them are in any particular order.

Arron Kosminski

Aaron Kosminski immigrated to Whitechapel in the early 1880s, sometime between either 1881 or 1882.[clii] Therefore, he lived in the Whitechapel area at the time of the murders and he would have had more than enough time to get very familiar with the area. Many experts believe Jack must have been a local who knew Whitechapel well. Well enough to get away and escape. He may also have been familiar with when the police done their patrols. Or, perhaps he wasn't even that calculated.

Kosminski was one of the many Polish Jews which immigrated to the East End of London in the late Victorian era. There was an increase in immigration due to the Tsar of Russia at the time perceiving people like Aaron to be 'the Jewish problem'.[cliii]

Poland was annexed by Russia at this point. The perception and treatment of Jews by the Tsarist regime, had caused many Jews to flee elsewhere, including London. The increase of Jewish immigration fuelled anti-Semitic behaviour and attitudes. It's thought that things like this and other additional things in Aaron's childhood, such as witnessing violence, could have made him immune to violence.[cliv]

It's also thought that his upbringing, probably contributed to him becoming mentally unstable. Just shortly after the Whitechapel Murders, coincidently around the same time as the last Whitechapel Murder, Kosminski was sent to Coleny Hatch Asylum in February 189[clv] any-more. The time-frame certainly fits with Aaron, he moved to Whitechapel just a few years before the murders took place, then he was sent to a mental asylum just when the murders came to an end. But that alone isn't enough to say that Aaron Kosminski was Jack the Ripper, we need more. And we have more.

There were a total of three senior police officers who believed that Kosminski was Jack the Ripper.[clvi] Those three police officials were Melville Macnaughten, Robert Anderson and Donald Swanson.[clvii] Given that these police officials would have had first-hand knowledge of the case and more information than is known to the public today, they would have had a better insight into who Jack the Ripper was.

In 1901, Robert Swanson also said that Jack the Ripper was placed in an asylum.[clviii] This would fit with what we know about Aaron Kosminski; that he was placed in an asylum. Kosminski couldn't have been brought justice. This was because, according to Swanson, that although Jack the Ripper was caught in the act and seen by one person, the same person wouldn't testify against him.

This is because the man was also a Jew. He stated that Jews don't testify against other Jews.[clix] Kosminski couldn't be brought to justice, because the witness wasn't willing to testify, according to Anderson. Swanson confirms that Kosminsi was the suspect.

Whereas, Melville goes further, he gives us an insight as to why Aaron Kosminski could have committed the crimes. He stated that Kosminski was insane and that he had a hatred from women, particularly prostitutes.[clx] This would be a strong motive for Kosminski. With Melville giving us this information, he provides us with a motive for this suspect – a hatred for prostitutes.

It seems like we have our suspect, we've found Jack the Ripper in Kosminski, right? Not really. There are arguments against Kosminski. The obvious one is that there is a lack of physical evidence. It doesn't exist. We sort of have evidence that Kosmski was caught in the act, however, given the witness unwilling to testify, it lacks substance.

Melville also had named two other suspects he thought were likely to have been Jack the Ripper. He stated that Kosminski was most likely. But, if he was certain, he wouldn't have named other suspects, so, he seems hesitant.

Finally, Kosminski while in in the asylum, didn't show any evidence of being murderous. He attacked someone with a chair[clxi] which shows that he was prone to violence. However, why was this the only instance of violence. It assumes that we are supposed to believe that Jack went from a murderous mutilator, to a chair thrower?

It doesn't really seem convincing.

There are two possible explanations for this. Either, he was so far gone, that Kosminski just wasn't mentally aware anymore. Or, we are looking at the wrong Kosminski and there was another one. Both seem as plausible.

Given that Jack the Ripper was out of control on the night of the Double Event and he hacked poor Mary Jane Kelly beyond recognition, in a violent rage. It shows signs that Jack the Ripper mentally snapped. So, it's possible, if Kosminski was the killer, that he just snapped. And by the time he was incarcerated, he wasn't even mentally aware anymore.

William Bury

The next suspect on our list, is William Bury. William Bury was a convicted killer, he killed his own wife just shortly after the Autumn of Terror, in Dundee.[clxii] He moved to the Whitechapel area of London in 1887.[clxiii] He married a prostitute called Ellen Elliot in April 1888. Bury was notably violent and abusive to his wife. He was caught threatening to slash his wife throat by their landlord.[clxiv] This provides evidence to us that William Bury was a violent character and he had the intent of murder. Two things needed in our suspect for Jack the Ripper.

William Bury was suspected at the time of being Jack the Ripper, apparently due to the similarities with how he murdered his wife and the women who were murdered by Jack the Ripper.[clxv] These similarities were taken so seriously, that they sent Inspector Abberline of the case, up to Scotland in 1889 to investigate it.[clxvi]

There's also the case that in William Bury's basement when he got to Scotland, that the words, 'Jack the Ripper is in this basement', were written.[clxvii] Additionally, it's reported that Ellen said to her neighbours that 'Jack the Ripper is having a rest now.'[clxviii] It seems significant, because we have to wonder, why would these things be made up?

What we can say, is that other people 'confessed' to being Jack the Ripper at the time. So, they can't all be right. Perhaps we can see why someone who committed a crime would have said these things. Perhaps they wanted notoriety or wanted some sick attention given to them. They got it, as they have lived through history with this case.

But, why did Ellen herself say it? What would she gain from it? Maybe she was just messed up emotionally. Or, maybe she thought that William was Jack the Ripper. Maybe she wanted to get revenge on him, because of his behaviour. But, what about the wall? Nothing seems to be gained from the writing on the wall, that probably only William and Ellen saw. Perhaps there is something to it, or perhaps there is nothing to it.

Interestingly, there was a message written on a wall in the night of the Double Event. That could or could not have been from Jack the Ripper. It would draw another similarity to William and Jack. However, like Kosminski, there isn't any evidence to say that William Bury was Jack the Ripper. The evidence is circumstantial at best. It should be noted that William Bury wasn't taken seriously as a candidate as Jack the Ripper.[clxix]

Inspect Abberline, the chief inspector of the Jack the Ripper case, went up to Dundee when William Bury murdered his wife. He was there to inspect whether William Bury was Jack the Ripper. He came back down to London, as he wasn't convinced William was Jack the Ripper. Perhaps this alone should rule out William Bury as a suspect.

Montague Druitt

One of the Jack the Ripper suspects which was taken more seriously by the police at the time of the Ripper events, was a man named Montague Druitt, who was named by Melville Macnaghten, in the Macnaghten Memoranda.[clxx]

What should be noted is, is that the Macnaughten Memoranda was written a few years after the Jack the Ripper murders had stopped, in 1894. The Canonical Five murders stopped in November 1888 and the Whitechapel Murders stopped in February 1891.

Melville wasn't part of the Ripper investigation at the time of the murders happening, he joined a few months later in the following year, June 1889.[clxxi] Therefore, he may not have had the first-hand knowledge that senior police officials did at the time of the Ripper murders. But, we cannot dismiss him, he would have had significant knowledge of the case. This makes his theories about the identity of the ripper credible.

For Macnaughten, he names three suspects, one of which is Druitt. So, who was Montague Druitt? And why was he suspected to being Jack the Ripper?

Druitt had various occupations, such as working at a school, in a bar and intended to focus on law to. Druitt, who's location from a census is revealed as Dorset, England.[clxxii] He moved to London at some point, it's unclear when he made this move.

One of the reasons given for Macnaughten to suspect Druitt, was that Druitt's suicide happened just shortly after the Jack the Ripper murders. The last Jack the Ripper murder happened on the 9th of November 1888 and Druitt was thought to have committed suicide in early December 1888.

It's unclear exactly when Druitt committed suicide, though, his body was found in the River Thames on New Years Eve 1888.[clxxiii] The timing of his death is suspicious and would offer us an explanation as to why the Jack the Ripper murders stopped. However, this alone isn't enough to say that Druitt was Jack the Ripper, we need more.

Another reason why Druitt was suspected, according to Macnaughten, was that he believed that Druitt's family members thought he was Jack the Ripper.[clxxiv] However, there is no evidence given that Druitt was Jack the Ripper.

In saying that, Druitt's family saying that he was Jack the Ripper, is not something we should dismiss lightly. We have to wonder why they suspected him of being Jack the Ripper? But, we also have others who claim to say that their family was also Jack, including William Bury's wife claiming that her husband being Jack the Ripper.

Then, we have others who claimed that they were Jack the Ripper. When we take it in this context, the allegations against Druitt seem to be much more complex. Not everyone who claimed to be Jack the Ripper, or everyone who was suspected of being Jack the

Ripper, can be Jack the Ripper. Only one of them can be.

So, either all of them are lying, or one of them is telling the truth. The fact that most of them are lying, indicates we should be sceptical of those who claimed to be Jack. Or accused of being Jack. We should treat these 'confessions' like the ripper letters, most 'confessions' are hoaxes. If Jack was only one man, then most of them have to be.

Many people being accused of being Jack the Ripper, it has contributed to the mystery of who Jack the Ripper was. What is clear, is that we don't know what exactly Macnaughten did know. Although we have the Macnaughten Memoranda, we don't have accessed to everything that Melville did, as he claimed he destroyed some of the papers available to him.[clxxv] Therefore, we don't know what exactly he knew.

In an interview with the Daily Mail, Melville said:

"Of course he was a maniac, but I have a very clear idea of who he was and how he committed suicide, but that, with other secrets, will never be revealed by me. I have destroyed all of my documents and there is now no record of the secret information which came into my possession at one time or another."[clxxvi]

It's suspicious that Melville destroyed evidence that he allegedly had. Why would he do that? Why would he destroy evidence in a murder case? And what other secrets and secret information did he know? Why did he have to destroy these secrets?

What is clear is that Melville had knowledge that we don't have today, if we believe what he was saying to the Daily Mail. Which means, there's something that he knew, that we don't today. Whether that information Melville had was legitimate or not, we will now never know. What is apparent, is that other police officers at the time disagreed with Melville about Melville's favoured suspect Druitt.

A few years after the memoranda was published, another senior police official, Inspector Abberline, gave an interview to the Pall Mall Gazette in 1903.[clxxvii] In that interview, he refuted the claim that Druitt was Jack the Ripper. This is some of what Inspector Abberline said to the Pall Mall Gazette in 1903:

"I know all about that story. But what does it amount to? Simply this. Soon after the last murder in Whitechapel the body of a young doctor was found in the Thames, but there is absolutely nothing beyond that fact that he was found at the time to incriminate him."[clxxviii]

Inspector Abberline did not believe that Druitt was Jack the Ripper, he believed that there were many theories about the killer's true identity. He said that the police were 'lost in theories' about the killer.[clxxix] [6] He also had other theories about who the killer was. Clearly, there was a disagreement with police officers at the time, of who they believed that Jack the Ripper was. Given that we don't know what else Melville knew, it's hard to make a judgement about which one of these two men were right.

In the next chapter, we are going to look at who the senior police officers at the time thought Jack the Ripper was. You already have an idea about what two of them thought. But, before we get on to that chapter, let's round up our suspects chapter, as there were many more suspects. We have only gone through a handful of suspects because there are literally hundreds of suspects accused of being Jack the Ripper.

You could write a whole book alone on the Jack the Ripper suspects alone. Suspects range from theories such as Jill the Ripper, to the painter Walter Sickert.

Some claim that Jack the Ripper wasn't a man at all. Some claim that Jack, was in fact a woman, hence the name Jill the Ripper. It would explain why the ripper wasn't caught. If they were looking for a man, and not a woman at the time, then a woman would have easily been looked over as being Jack the Ripper.

The problem with this theory, is that every eye witness who saw the victims last, said that they saw the women with another man. Which suggests that the ripper was a man.

Walter Sickert is an interesting character, to put it politely. Walter had a keen interest in Jack the Ripper. He was morbidly interested in the case. He even drew a creepy drawing called 'Jack the Ripper's Bedroom.' And also he drew a painting which eerily looks like the last Jack the Ripper murder, the murder of Mary Jane Kelly. Walter Sickert is a weird and interesting character.... could he have been Jack the Ripper?

There have been literally, hundreds of people accused of being Jack the Ripper. In fact, you would probably be quicker naming the people of the time the murders were committed, who *weren't* accused of being Jack the Ripper. It looks like anyone and every-one who was alive during this era, has been accused of being Jack the Ripper.

Our next chapter is not going to look at all of these suspects. Instead, the next chapter is going to look at the suspects the police thought was Jack the Ripper.

CHAPTER SEVEN: JACK THE RIPPER: THE POLICE'S FAVOURED SUSPECTS

One of the reasons we have so many suspects today and, making the case a bigger mystery (than is perhaps necessary), is the police themselves had different opinions as to who Jack the Ripper was.

The police were conflicted as to who Jack the Ripper was. Senior police officers at the time of the murders, had different views and opinions to who they believed Jack the Ripper was. The police would have had a better insight into the case than we do today, considering that they would have had first hand knowledge, and they also knew stuff that we didn't (considering that there has been a lot of information destroyed).

The senior officials at the time of the Jack the Ripper murders, would have had first-hand knowledge of the case; they would have known better than what we do today about the case. This is because much of the original official documents have been destroyed. Other files have been hidden from the public.

We have to go on the information that *is* available to us. So, let's take a look at who the senior officials thought was Jack the Ripper.

Inspector Abberline

Inspector Abberline was the chief inspector of the case, he was the leading man leading the search for Jack the Ripper. Inspector Abberline thought that a man called George Chapman was Jack the Ripper.[clxxx] Abberline said in the interview with the Pall Mall Gazette in 1903 that "..I cannot help feeling that this is the man we struggled so hard to find fifteen years ago."[clxxxi] That man he thought of, was George Chapman.

Sir Robert Anderson

Sir Robert Anderson was another senior official in the Jack the Ripper case at the time of the murders, he doesn't think that George Chapman is the killer. Instead, Anderson said that the killer was known to the police. He didn't name the killer directly, but it's assumed that he meant that Jack the Ripper was Aaron Kosminski.[clxxxii]

Donald Swanson

Senior officer at the time of the Ripper murders Donald Swanson agreed with Anderson; he favoured Aaron Kosminski as the killer and therefore, Jack the Ripper. Swanson directly said that Kosminski was Jack the Ripper, that he was sent to an asylum and he died shortly afterwards.[clxxxiii] So far, we have two out of three senior officers favouring Aaron Kosminski as being Jack the Ripper. What about our fourth and final?

Melville Macnaughten

Melville also named Kosminski as one of his suspects. But, he two other suspects, Druitt, as we have already said, who was his favoured suspect. He also named a man called Michael Ostrog, as being one of his favoured suspects for Jack the Ripper.

Conclusion

All of the senior police officers, except Abberline, suspected Aaron Kosminski of being Jack the Ripper. We can conclude that the police favoured Kosminksi as being Jack the Ripper. However, we can also conclude that they disagreed with each other about the killer. If the police at the time couldn't even agree on who Jack the Ripper was, it's no wonder that Jack the Ripper's true identity remains a mystery to this day.

CHAPTER EIGHT:
WHO WAS JACK
THE RIPPER?

There are several suspects which are more interesting than others, such as Kosminski, Bury and Sickert. These are the three suspects which stand out the most. The problem with this case though, is that the evidence is either circumstantial or that it is non-existent when it comes to a suspect. There is a lack of evidence in this case, but that is what makes it interesting and mysterious.

If we knew that Jack the Ripper was Joe Doe, then, we wouldn't even be discussing the case, it would have likely have been lost in historical obscurity. It is the mystery surrounding Jack the Ripper that draws us to this case – it is the ultimate 'who dunnit'.

But, it is a who dunnit that probably will never be solved, unless we find new evidence or new technology that enlightens us to who it was. Unless we stumble upon new evidence, or new technology, then most likely, we will be wondering who Jack the Ripper was forever. There doesn't seem to be any hope at finding out the truth.

Although new evidence could show up at any time, it's highly unlikely that it will. Far too much time has passed since the ripper events happened, so the prospect of physical evidence showing up seems to be non-existent. Even if we did find physical evidence, by this point it's probably been cross-contaminated so many times, that it would be worthless. That means that any new light on this case, would have to come from technology. For now, though, we have to go on the information that's available.

There is one last suspect that we should consider. A theory that is often overlooked, or ignored, when it comes to Jack the Ripper. That theory is, what if Jack the Ripper has been lost in historical obscurity? What if the reason we haven't found out who he was, is not because of the lack of evidence towards any known suspect. But because none of the suspects on the list is Jack the Ripper. Jack the Ripper could be unknown.

It would make sense. It would make sense that the reason none of the known suspects have been officially confirmed as Jack the Ripper, is because none of them are Jack the Ripper. The reason there's no real tangible evidence to link any of these, is, or might be because we have been looking for the suspect in the wrong place.

What if Jack the Ripper is a man, an ordinary man from White-chapel, who evaded the police at the time. A man who has never been identified, a man who isn't known to the history books, because there was no reason to suspect him.

If we found out who Jack the Ripper was tomorrow, our reaction might be *'who..?',* rather than *'I told you so!'*

If we can say anything with certainty, it's that we are none the wiser as to who Jack the Ripper was 130 years on. The most honest answer to, 'Who was Jack the Ripper?' is, 'We don't have a clue who Jack the Ripper was. We probably never will know who Jack the Ripper was.' In 130 years into the future, the mystery will probably still remain a mystery.

CONCLUSION

Jack the Ripper was a notorious Victorian serial killer, who killed at least five women. Possibly he killed six women. The number of women he killed could have been higher.

The Canonical Five victims were thought to have been murder by Jack the Ripper. They were murdered in the Autumn of 1888. There were also several letters sent during the Autumn of 1888 to the police. The most infamous of these letters was, the Dear Boss letter, the From Hell letter, and the Saucy Jack Postcard.

Two of these letters, the Dear Boss letter and the Saucy Jack post card, were most likely hoaxes. The From Hell letter, sent to it's recipient with half a human kidney, was probably the only authentic letter. There were hundreds of other letters sent.

The Whitechapel Murders lasted from April 1888 to February 1891. It included eleven murdered women in total. Today, most of these women were not thought to have been murdered by Jack the Ripper. Though, all of them at one point or another, have been suspected of being done by Jack the Ripper.

The police at the time didn't catch the killers of the other women. They neither captured Jack the Ripper. On the night of the Double Event, Jack the Ripper was almost caught. It's possible that he just evaded police during the murder of Mary Ann Nichols (who was still warm when found), and Catherine Eddowes, who had been found several minutes just after her murder. Either the ripper was very lucky, or, he knew how to avoid the police. Perhaps he was in the police force, which is how he evaded capture?

There is a lot of speculation as to who Jack the Ripper was. Today, 130 years on from the Whitechapel Murders, we are still speculating who Jack the Ripper was. One hundred and thirty years on, and we still don't know who the ripper was.

Bibliography

[i] MJ Trow, Ripper Hunter: Abberline and the Whitechapel Murders, 2012, (n.p)

[ii] Accessed on the 21st of November 2017, http://www.casebook.org/victims/millwood.html

[iii] Accessed on the 21st of November 2017, http://www.casebook.org/victims/millwood.html

[iv] Accessed on the 2nd of January 2018, https://www.jack-the-ripper-tour.com/generalnews/possible-early-jack-the-ripper-victim/

[v] Accessed on the 21st of November 2017, http://www.casebook.org/victims/adawils.html

[vi] Accessed on the 2nd of January 2018, https://www.jack-the-ripper-tour.com/generalnews/was-this-an-early-jack-the-ripper-attack/

[vii] Peter Rutt, Jack the Ripper: From Cradle to the Grave, Pg 98

[viii] Nigel Weir, British Serial Killers, Pg 78

[ix] Andrew Cook, Jack the Ripper, 2009, Pg 36

[x] Accessed on the 2nd of January 2018, http://www.casebook.org/victims/tabram.html

[xi] John Marriott, Beyond the Tower: A history of the East End of London, Pg 150

[xii] Accessed on the 17th of January 2018 https://www.jack-the-ripper-tour.com/the-victims/

[xiii] Accessed on the 17th of January 2018 http://www.casebook.org/victims/polly.html

[xiv] Accessed on the 17th of January 2018 http://www.casebook.org/victims/polly.html

[xv] Accessed on the 17th of January 2018 http://www.casebook.org/victims/chapman.html

[xvi] Accessed on the 17th of January 2018 http://www.casebook.org/victims/chapman.html

[xvii] Accessed on the 19th of January 2018 https://www.jack-the-ripper-tour.com/generalnews/jack-the-ripper-where-did-he-come-from/

Jennifer Helen Johnstone

[xviii] Accessed on the 19th of January 2018 https://www.jack-the-ripper-tour.com/generalnews/the-30th-september-1888-double-event/

[xix] Accessed on the 19th of January 2018 http://www.jack-the-ripper.org/goulston-street-graffito.htm

[xx]

[xxi] John J Eddleston, Jack the Ripper: An Encyclopaedia, Pg158, 2001.

[xxii] Donald Rumbelow, Complete Jack the Ripper, Pg121, 2016

[xxiii] Accessed on the 22nd of February 2018 https://www.jack-the-ripper-tour.com/letters-from-the-ripper/

[xxiv] Accessed on the 22nd of February 2018 https://www.jack-the-ripper-tour.com/letters-from-the-ripper/

[xxv] Terry Lynch, Jack the Ripper, Pg83, 2008

[xxvi] Accessed on the 22nd of February 2018 https://www.jack-the-ripper-tour.com/generalnews/a-quick-look-at-the-jack-the-ripper-case/

[xxvii] Accessed on the 28th of February 2018 http://www.casebook.org/victims/mylett.html

[xxviii] Accessed on the 28th of February 2018 http://www.casebook.org/victims/mckenzie.html

[xxix] G. Alexander, Jack the Ripper: Case Solved?, Pg68, 2015

[xxx] Accessed on the 28th of February 2018 http://www.casebook.org/victims/pinchin.html

[xxxi] Nigel Wier, British Serial Killers, Pg79, 2011

[xxxii] Accessed on the 1st of March 2018 http://www.casebook.org/

[xxxiii] Accessed on the 1st of March 2018 http://www.casebook.org/dissertations/dst-strd.html

[xxxiv] Accessed on the 1st of March 2018 http://www.casebook.org/witnesses/w/Louis_Diemschutz.html

[xxxv] Mark Barresi, The Reckoning of Jack the Ripper: Entity Unknown, Pg35, 2012

[xxxvi] Paul Begg, Jack the Ripper; The Definitive History, Pg105, 2013

[xxxvii] Paul Begg, Jack the Ripper: The Definitive History, Pg105, 2013

[xxxviii] Paul Begg, Martin Fido, Keith Skinner, The Complete Jack the Ripper Book A-Z,

[xxxix] Accessed on the 1st of March 2018 http://www.casebook.org/victims/polly.html

[xl] Accessed on the 1st of March 2018 http://www.casebook.org/victims/polly.html

[xli] Peter Hodgson, Jack the Ripper – Through the Mists of Time, Pg18, 2011

[xlii] Accessed on the 2nd of March 2018 http://www.casebook.org/victims/polly.html

[xliii] Paul Begg, Martin Fido, Keith Skinner, The Complete Jack the Ripper A-Z The Ultimate Guide To The Ripper, Pg15, 2015

[xliv] Accessed on the 2nd of March http://www.casebook.org/victims/polly.html

[xlv] Accessed on the 8th of March 2018 http://www.casebook.org/victims/chapman.html

[xlvi] John J Eddlestone, Jack the Ripper: An Enclopedia, Pg99, 2001

[xlvii] Accessed on the 21st of November 2017 http://www.casebook.org/victims/chapman.html

[xlviii] The Complete Jack the Ripper Guide A-Z – The ultimate guide to the Ripper mystery, section Annie Chapman (1841-1888), by Begg, Fido and Skinner.

[xlix] Accessed on the 21st of November 2017 http://www.victorianweb.org/economics/wages4.html

[l] Accessed on the 21st of November 2017 http://www.casebook.org/witnesses/w/Eliza_Cooper.html

[li] Accessed on the 21st of November 2017 http://www.casebook.org/suspects/jill.html

[lii] Accessed on the 21st of November 2017 http://www.casebook.org/witnesses/w/Eliza_Cooper.html

[liii] Accessed on the 21st of November 2017 http://www.casebook.org/victims/chapman.html

[liv] Accessed on the 21st of November 2017 http://www.casebook.org/witnesses/w/Amelia_Palmer.html

[lv] Accessed on the 21st of November 1888 http://www.casebook.org/victims/chapman.html

[lvi] Accessed on the 21st of November 2017 http://www.casebook.org/victims/chapman.html

[lvii] Accessed on the 21st of November 2017 http://www.casebook.org/victims/chapman.html

[lviii] Accessed on the 21st of November 2017 http://www.casebook.org/victims/chapman.html

[lix] Accessed on the 21st of November 2017 http://www.casebook.org/victims/chapman.html

[lx] Accessed the 21st of November 2017 http://www.casebook.org/ripper_media/book_reviews/non-fiction/cjmorley/51.html

[lxi] Accessed the 21st of November 2017 http://www.casebook.org/ripper_media/book_reviews/non-fiction/cjmorley/51.html

[lxii] Accessed on the 21st of November 2017 http://www.casebook.org/victims/tabram.html

[lxiii] Accessed the 21st of November 2017 http://www.casebook.org/ripper_media/book_reviews/non-fiction/cjmorley/51.html

[lxiv] Accessed the 25th of November 2017 http://www.casebook.org/witnesses/w/John_Davis.html

[lxv] Accessed the 25th of November 2017 http://www.casebook.org/witnesses/w/John_Davis.html

[lxvi] John J. Eddleston, Jack the Ripper: An encyclopaedia, Pg182, 2001

[lxvii] John J. Eddleston, Jack the Ripper: An encyclopaedia, Pg232, 2001

[lxviii] Accessed on the 25th of November 2017 http://www.casebook.org/victims/stride.html

[lxix] Accessed on the 25th of November 2017 http://www.casebook.org/victims/stride.html

[lxx] Accessed on the 25th of November 2017 http://www.casebook.org/victims/stride.html

[lxxi] Accessed on the 29th of November 2017 http://www.jack-the-ripper.org/dear-boss.htm

[lxxii] Accessed on the 29th of November 2017 https://www.jack-the-ripper-tour.com/leather-apron/

[lxxiii] Accessed on the 29th of November 2017 http://www.casebook.org/press_reports/star/s880905.html

[lxxiv] Accessed on the 29th of November 2017 http://www.casebook.org/victims/stride.html

[lxxv] Accessed on the 29th of November 2017 http://www.casebook.org/victims/stride.html

[lxxvi] Accessed on the 6th of December 2017 http://www.casebook.org/victims/stride.html

[lxxvii] Accessed on the 6th of December 2017 http://www.casebook.org/victims/stride.html

[lxxviii] Accessed on the 6th of December 2017 http://www.casebook.org/victims/stride.html

[lxxix] Accessed on the 6th of December 2017 http://www.casebook.org/victims/stride.html

[lxxx]

[lxxxi] Victor Stapleton, Jack the Ripper: The Murders, the Mystery, the Myth, Pg23, 2014

[lxxxii] Accessed on the 6th of December 2017 http://www.casebook.org/victims/eddowes.html

[lxxxiii] Accessed on the 6th of December 2017 http://www.casebook.org/victims/eddowes.html

[lxxxiv] Accessed on the 6th of September 1888 https://www.jack-the-ripper-tour.com/generalnews/the-catherine-eddowes-murder-mitre-square/

[lxxxv] Alex Binney, Demons, Pg174, 2012

[lxxxvi] Accessed on the 7th of December 2017 https://www.jack-the-ripper-tour.com/generalnews/the-catherine-eddowes-murder-mitre-square/

[lxxxvii] Accessed on the 7th of December 2017 http://www.casebook.org/dissertations/dst-graffito.html

[lxxxviii] Accessed on the 7th of December 1888 http://www.casebook.org/dissertations/dst-graffito.html

[lxxxix] Accessed on the 7th of December 2017 http://www.jack-the-ripper.org/goulston-street-graffito.htm

[xc] Accessed on the 7th of December 2017 http://www.jack-the-ripper.org/goulston-street-graffito.htm

[xci] Accessed on the 7th of December 2017 http://www.jack-the-ripper.org/jewish-history.htm

[xcii] Accessed on the 7th of December 2017 https://www.jack-the-ripper-tour.com/generalnews/ripper-riots/

[xciii] Accessed on the 7th of December 2017 https://www.bl.uk/collection-items/suspicious-characters-from-the-illustrated-london-news

[xciv] Accessed on the 8th of December 2017 http://www.casebook.org/victims/mary_jane_kelly.html

[xcv] Paul Begg, Jack the Ripper: The Facts, Pg279, 2005

[xcvi] Accessed on the 8th of November 1888 http://www.casebook.org/official_documents/inquests/inquest_kelly.html

[xcvii] Accessed on the 8th of November 1888 http://www.casebook.org/victims/mary_jane_kelly.html

[xcviii] Accessed on the 8th of November 1888 http://www.thejacktherippertour.com/blog/will-the-real-mary-jane-kelly-please-stand-up/

[xcix] Accessed on the 8th of December 2017 https://www.jack-the-ripper-tour.com/generalnews/another-year-another-suspect/

[c] Accessed on the 8th of December 2017 https://www.thejacktheripperwalk.com/story-mary-kelly/

[ci] Accessed on the 8th of December 2017 https://www.thejacktheripperwalk.com/story-mary-kelly/

[cii] Accessed on the 8th of December 2017 https://www.thejacktheripperwalk.com/story-mary-kelly/

[ciii] Accessed on the 8th of December 2017 https://www.thejacktheripperwalk.com/story-mary-kelly/

[civ] Accessed on the 8th of December 2017 http://www.casebook.org/witnesses/w/Elizabeth_Prater.html

[cv] Accessed on the 8th of December 2017 http://www.casebook.org/witnesses/w/Elizabeth_Prater.html

[cvi] Accessed on the 8th of December 2017 https://www.thejacktheripperwalk.com/story-mary-kelly/

[cvii] Accessed on the 8th of December 2017 http://www.casebook.org/victims/mary_jane_kelly.html

[cviii] Accessed on the 8th of December 2017 http://www.casebook.org/victims/mary_jane_kelly.html

[cix] Accessed on the 8th of December 2017 http://www.casebook.org/victims/mary_jane_kelly.html

[cx] Accessed on the 8th of December 2017 http://www.casebook.org/victims/mary_jane_kelly.html

[cxi] Accessed on the 8th of December 2017 http://www.casebook.org/victims/mary_jane_kelly.html

[cxii] Paul Begg, Jack the Ripper: The Definitive History, Pg305, 2013

[cxiii] Accessed on the 13th of December 2017 http://www.casebook.org/dissertations/ripperoo-todeath.html

[cxiv] John J. Eddleston, Jack the Ripper: An Encyclopaedia, Pg61, 2001

[cxv] Accessed on the 13th of December 2017 https://www.jack-the-ripper-tour.com/history/

[cxvi] Andrew Cook, Jack the Ripper, Pg151, 2009

[cxvii] Accessed on the 13th of December 2017 http://www.jack-the-ripper-walk.co.uk/victims.htm

[cxviii] Alan Moore, Eddie Campbell, From Hell, Pg8, 1989

[cxix] Alan Moss, Keith Skinner, The Scotland Yard Files: Milestones in Crime Deception, Pg103, 2006

[cxx] John J. Eddleston, Jack the Ripper: An Encyclopedia, Pg86, 2001

[cxxi] Accessed on the 14th of December 2017 http://www.casebook.org/victims/tabram.html

Jennifer Helen Johnstone

[cxxii] Accessed on the 14th of December 2017 http://www.casebook.org/victims/tabram.html

[cxxiii] Accessed on the 14th of December 2017 http://www.casebook.org/victims/tabram.html

[cxxiv] Accessed on the 14th of December 2017 http://www.casebook.org/victims/mylett.html

[cxxv] Accessed on the 14th of December 2017 http://www.casebook.org/victims/mylett.html

[cxxvi] Accessed on the 14th of December 2017 http://www.casebook.org/victims/mylett.html

[cxxvii] Accessed on the 14th of December 2017 http://www.victorianweb.org/history/slums.html

[cxxviii] Accessed on the 14th of December 2017 http://www.thejacktherippertour.com/blog/what-was-it-really-like-to-live-in-whitechapel-london-in-1888/

[cxxix] Accessed on the 14th of December 2017 http://www.thejacktherippertour.com/blog/what-was-it-really-like-to-live-in-whitechapel-london-in-1888/

[cxxx] Accessed on the 17th of December 2017 http://www.casebook.org/press_reports/

[cxxxi] Accessed on the 17th of December 2017 http://www.casebook.org/press_reports/

[cxxxii] Accessed on the 17th of December 2017 http://dickens.port.ac.uk/poverty/

[cxxxiii] Accessed on the 17th of December 2017 https://artscolumbia.org/literary-arts/prose/christmas-carol-charles-dickens-2-20487/

[cxxxiv] Accessed on the 17th of December https://victorianchildren.org/victorian-schools/

[cxxxv] Accessed on the 17th of December https://victorianchildren.org/victorian-schools/

[cxxxvi] Accessed on the 17th of December 2017 https://www.jrf.org.uk/sites/default/files/jrf/migrated/files/2123.pdf

[cxxxvii] Accessed on the 17th of December 2017 http://www.casebook.org/ripper_letters/

[cxxxviii] Accessed on the 17th of December 2017 https://whitechapeljack.com/the-ripper-letters/

[cxxxix] Accessed on the 18th of December 2017 https://www2.le.ac.uk/offices/press/features/features-2017/mary-jane-kelly/jack-the-ripper

[cxl] Accessed on the 18th of December 2017 https://whitechapeljack.com/whitechapel-vigilance-committee/

[cxli] Accessed on the 18th of December 2017 https://whitechapeljack.com/whitechapel-vigilance-committee/

[cxlii] Accessed on the 18th of December 2017 https://www.bl.uk/collection-items/suspicious-characters-from-the-illustrated-london-news

[cxliii] Accessed on the 18th of December 2017 http://www.casebook.org/ripper_letters/

[cxliv] Accessed on the 18th of December 2017 https://www.jack-the-ripper-tour.com/generalnews/a-jack-the-ripper-location/

[cxlv] Accessed on the 18th of December http://www.casebook.org/dissertations/dst-cmdlusk.html

[cxlvi] Accessed on the 18th of December https://www.jack-the-ripper-tour.com/generalnews/mr-lusk-gets-a-stalker/

[cxlvii] Accessed on the 18th of December 2017 http://www.jack-the-ripper-walk.co.uk/the-dear-boss-letter.htm

[cxlviii] Accessed on the 18th of December 2017 https://blog.britishnewspaperarchive.co.uk/2014/09/18/%E2%80%98dear-boss%E2%80%99-letter-how-jack-the-ripper-got-his-name/

[cxlix] Accessed on the 18th of December 2017

https://blog.britishnewspaperarchive.co.uk/2014/09/18/%E2%80%98dear-boss%E2%80%99-letter-how-jack-the-ripper-got-his-name/

[cl] Accessed on the 14th of March 2018 http://www.bbc.co.uk/news/uk-england-london-42901781

[cli] Accessed on the 18th of December 2017 http://www.casebook.org/ripper_letters/

[clii] Accessed on the 19th of December 2017 http://www.casebook.org/dissertations/robhouse-kosminski.html

[cliii] Accessed on the 19th of December 2017 http://www.casebook.org/dissertations/robhouse-kosminski.html

[cliv] Accessed on the 19th of December 2017 http://www.casebook.org/dissertations/robhouse-kosminski.html

[clv] Accessed on the 19th of December 2017 http://www.jack-the-ripper.org/kosminski.htm

[clvi] Accessed on the 19th of December 2017 http://www.jack-the-ripper.org/kosminski.htm

[clvii] Accessed on the 19th of December 2017 http://www.casebook.org/ripper_media/book_reviews/non-fiction/cjmorley/107.html

[clviii] Accessed on the 19th of December 2017 http://www.casebook.org/ripper_media/book_reviews/non-fiction/cjmorley/107.html

[clix] Accessed on the 19th of December 2017 http://www.casebook.org/ripper_media/book_reviews/non-fiction/cjmorley/107.html

[clx] Accessed on the 18th of December 2017 http://www.jack-the-ripper.org/kosminski.htm

[clxi] Accessed on the 19th of December 2017 http://www.casebook.org/ripper_media/book_reviews/non-fiction/cjmorley/107.html

[clxii] Accessed on the 19th of December 2017 http://www.casebook.org/suspects/bury.html

[clxiii] Accessed on the 19th of December 2017 http://www.thejacktherippertour.com/blog/spotlight-on-william-bury/

[clxiv] Accessed on the 19th of December 2017 http://www.thejacktherippertour.com/blog/spotlight-on-william-bury/

[clxv] Accessed on the 19th of December 2017 http://www.casebook.org/suspects/bury.html

[clxvi] Accessed on the 19th of December 2017 http://www.casebook.org/suspects/bury.html

[clxvii] Accessed on the 19th of December 2017 http://www.casebook.org/suspects/bury.html

[clxviii] Accessed on the 19th of December 2017 http://www.casebook.org/suspects/bury.html

[clxix] Accessed on the 19th of December 2017 http://www.casebook.org/suspects/bury.html

[clxx] Jack the Ripper Encyclopaedia, By John J. Eddleston, Page 127.

[clxxi] Accessed on the 27th of December 2017 Jack the Ripper Encyclopaedia, By John J. Eddleston, Page 127.

[clxxii] Accessed on the 27th of December 2017 http://www.casebook.org/suspects/druitt.html

[clxxiii] Accessed on the 27th of December 1888 http://www.jack-the-ripper.org/druitt.htm

[clxxiv] Accessed on the 27th of December 2017 http://www.casebook.org/suspects/druitt.html

[clxxv] Accessed on the 27th of December 2017 https://www.jack-the-ripper-tour.com/ripper-suspects/

[clxxvi] Accessed on the 27th of December 2017 https://www.jack-the-ripper-tour.com/ripper-suspects/

[clxxvii] Accessed on the 27th of December 2017 http://www.jack-the-ripper.org/druitt.htm

[clxxviii] Accessed on the 27th of December 2017 http://www.jack-the-ripper.org/druitt.htm

[clxxix] Accessed on the 27th of December 2017 https://www.jack-the-ripper-tour.com/generalnews/lost-in-theories/

Jennifer Helen Johnstone

[clxxx] Accessed on the 27th of December 2017 http://www.casebook.org/police_officials/po-abber.html

[clxxxi] Accessed on the 27th of December 2017 http://www.casebook.org/police_officials/po-abber.html

[clxxxii] Accessed on the 27th of December 2017 http://www.casebook.org/police_officials/po-ander.html

[clxxxiii] Accessed on the 27th of December http://www.casebook.org/police_officials/po-swan.html

Printed in Great Britain
by Amazon